Freedom for His Princess

Books by Sheri Rose Shepherd

Fit for My King
His Princess Bride
His Princess Girl Talk with God
His Princess Warrior

Freedom for His Princess

30 Days to Refresh Your Soul

Sheri Rose Shepherd

Revell

a division of Baker Publishing Group
Grand Rapids, Michigan

Published by Revell
a division of Baker Publishing Group
P.O. Box 6287, Grand Rapids, MI 49516-6287
www.revellbooks.com

Printed in China

Library of Congress Cataloging-in-Publication Data
Shepherd, Sheri Rose, 1961–
    Freedom for his princess : 30 days to refresh your soul / Sheri Rose
Shepherd.
        p.   cm.
    ISBN 978-0-8007-1917-3 (cloth)
    1. Christian women—Prayers and devotions. 2. Liberty—Religious
aspects—Christianity—Prayers and devotions. I. Title.
BV4844.S5336 2012
242′.643—dc23   2011030660

12 13 14 15 16 17 18   7 6 5 4 3 2 1

I dedicate this book to all those
who have stood in the gap for me,
covered me in prayer,
and encouraged me to keep
writing and speaking.

CONTENTS

ACKNOWLEDGMENTS

I want to thank—

My husband, Steven, who has sent me out with his blessing to minister at women's conferences and retreats for over twenty years. Honey, you exemplify the heart of Jesus by the way you serve your family. Marriage can be hard, but we fought for each other and stand strong today.

My son, Jake, who has been by my side at more women's events than any son should have to attend. You served me, prayed over me, carried my luggage, set up my table, and lived on the road most of your growing-up years, yet you never complained about the call God put on your mother's life to minister.

My daughter-in-law, Amanda, who is the answer to my prayer for my son. You are a true Princess Warrior for God, and it is an honor to call you my daughter. Thank you for the way you love my son.

My surprise baby girl, Emilie, who came eleven years after my son, Jake. I adore you, Emilie Joy. Thank you for sharing your mommy with so many, for praying over me every time I speak, and for playing with me when I need some girl time. You define the words Princess Warrior, and I cannot wait to see what God is going to do with your life as you grow. I love having you travel with me, and you are a big part of this ministry.

A WORD FROM SHERI ROSE

> It is for freedom that Christ has set us free. Stand
> firm and do not let yourselves be burdened again by
> a yoke of slavery.
>
> GALATIANS 5:1 NIV

I have been teaching and speaking at women's retreats
and conferences for over twenty years and have discovered that many of us women know and love the Lord
but feel everything . . . but *free*!

I don't know what holds you back from freedom in
Christ, but I do know from personal experience what
it's like to feel powerless and defeated no matter how
hard I try to be strong.

I have walked through many painful places in my
life. I grew up in a dysfunctional home, my parents
have been married and divorced three times each, and
I've been a part of five blended families. When I needed
comfort, I found it in food. When I was in pain, I used
drugs and alcohol to escape. Eventually, I became addicted to both food and drugs. I had made so many
poor choices and burned so many bridges that I nearly

destroyed my mind and body. I believed I was destined for destruction. I wanted desperately to crawl out of this deep, dark hole of despair, but the harder I tried, the deeper I fell and the emptier I felt inside. Today, in God's strength and His truth, I am free in Christ. I must be honest, though, it has been a fight . . . but freedom is worth fighting for!

I don't know where your heart is at this moment or what season of life you are in. Maybe you're feeling extremely overwhelmed by your circumstances or life has hit you harder than you ever expected. I do know that many times life does not seem fair or just. I so wish I could give you a reason for every sad and awful thing that is happening in our world or to you personally and pray away all the pain this life can bring.

What I can give you in this "Freedom Book" you hold in your hands is thirty days of refreshment for your soul—thirty days of mentoring filled with treasures of truth, scriptural Love Letters, and Bible life coaching that I have discovered from twenty years in the Word, in women's ministry, and in my own life.

Together we will find the biblical keys to freedom and get an eternal look at our lives and our legacy as we learn to walk in the freedom our Savior gave His life for!

I am praying for you to experience blessings and breakthroughs in every area of your life!

SHERI ROSE

Fight the Good Fight
Run to God
Eliminate What Hinders You
Embrace Life's Battle
Do What God Asks You to Do
Operate in Your Appointed Position
Move On

1

FIGHT THE GOOD FIGHT

But you, Timothy, are a man of God; so run from all
these evil things. Pursue righteousness and a godly life,
along with faith, love, perseverance, and gentleness.

1 TIMOTHY 6:11

The first invitation I received to speak publicly came
from an unlikely person. She was a woman who I felt
had humiliated me at the dinner table in front of my
husband's Bible professors. There I was, already intimi-
dated by the educated people at this event, when one
of the women at our table said to me in a loud voice,
"I heard you used to be fat, Jewish, and on drugs. How
did you ever become a Christian?"

Of course all eyes were suddenly on me. I felt forced
at that point to share my life story in front of a table
of strangers. I am not proud of my life before Christ,
and every word felt like a fight as I struggled to explain

my sin and salvation experience. When they finally stopped asking questions, I excused myself to go to the bathroom, and there I begged God to never let that happen again.

That night as I crawled into bed, I played back my personal battles of regret, guilt, and shame. I did not feel worthy of sharing my faith. I wanted to hide my past and pretend it never happened. I know I am not the only person who struggles with feeling unworthy for God to use me to further His Kingdom on earth and who fights these inward battles of wanting to do something great for God.

It has been over twenty years since that humiliating moment, but when I look back, I now realize that was the moment God used to birth my speaking and writing ministry. That very woman, who humiliated me at dinner, later invited me to share my story in front of that entire group of Christian leaders. Those leaders invited me to share my story with their women's groups, and I have been invited to speak and write books ever since.

I did not ever dream I would be in ministry. But God has a strange way of calling each of us. Paul was blinded in order to see his true calling, and there is a Paul inside each of us. What I mean by that is that our heart screams to live a life of adventure and a life that makes a difference while we are here. That life is found in fighting to further God's Kingdom on earth.

You don't have to have a lot of faith to do great things in God's Kingdom. Just a little faith and a sweet surrender to God's calling will help you find the passion and power to fight.

TODAY'S BIBLE LIFE COACHING

I have fought the good fight, I have finished the race,
I have kept the faith.

2 TIMOTHY 4:7 NIV

In this Scripture, Paul is at the end of his life. He wants us to know what he has accomplished in his faith journey. He has fought, finished, and stayed faithful. As you know, Paul was not any more perfect than any of us, but God chose him anyway, even with all of his pride and imperfections. Wouldn't it be amazing to say at the end of our imperfect lives that we fought the good fight, finished our race, and kept our faith in spite of all our pain, disappointments, and inadequacies?

I know life can hit us so hard that there isn't any fight left inside us, and even on the best of days, we can find ourselves in the midst of a battle that attempts to steal our peace. Our Daddy in heaven understands the spiritual heat His daughters experience. He is aware of how hard it is to keep fighting when we are worn out and don't see the fruits of our efforts and energy. It's very tempting to walk off the battlefield and just give in to the weakness of our weary souls.

But when life is over, and all is said and done, there will be no better way to exit this earth into heaven than the way Paul did—fighting the good fight so the next generation has a faith to stand on.

Look at it this way: if we give up now, it is like planting a beautiful fruit tree and chopping it down before it is ready to bear fruit that we can see and taste. The Word of God promises a crown for those who finish their race. I can think of no better reward than to know our lives led many to the King of Kings, and our fight brought victory for our children and grandchildren.

I know you want to finish strong, so be encouraged with this truth.

It's never too late to get up and finish your faith fight and plant your feet in God's Word. It will produce great fruit in the next generation. Even if you are too weak to fight today, you can take the first step by standing; if you're too weak to stand, then kneel and call out to your Daddy in heaven. He loves you and is your faithful God.

His Princess Love Letter

I believe if your heavenly Father wrote you a personal love letter for today, it would read like this:

Beloved Princess . . .

Choose your battles. Every day can be a fight for something or with someone if you so choose. I want you, My Princess Warrior, to choose your battles wisely and fight for the things worth fighting for. The enemy of your soul will entice you to fight the wrong battles in order to distract you from your main mission. Remember, My beloved, your fight is not against flesh and blood, but against evil forces in the spiritual realm. When you find yourself in the midst of a war, do not be afraid. Call on Me in prayer and allow Me to deliver you. In My timing, I will give you the victory and bring justice. So don't waste your precious time fighting the wrong battles. And never forget that the spiritual war is fought and won on your knees.

Love,
 Your heavenly Father

TODAY'S *TREASURE* OF TRUTH

Even when you feel like you are in the middle of a war, the battle is not yours—it is the Lord's.

2

FIGHT FOR TRUTH

For I speak the truth and detest every kind of deception.
PROVERBS 8:7

When people ask me, as they often do, "How did you break free from your painful past, your poor choices, your food addiction, your insecurities and guilt and regret?" my answer is, "I had to fight." I had to fight the lies I believed about myself. I had to saturate myself with God's truth to find a true replacement for the lies.

I know what it is like to feel worthless and to have word curses spoken over you. When I was in high school, an English teacher walked up to me in front of all of my classmates and said, "Sheri Rose, you were born to lose in life. You will never, ever amount to anything." At that moment, I traded my dreams and hopes for the future for a lie that kept me locked up for years.

I know many of you reading this right now have just recognized the root of the lie you have been living in. If you haven't, take a moment to think it through. Maybe it comes from hurtful words spoken to you by a father or mother, brother or sister, teacher, boyfriend or husband. Maybe it was a stranger who thoughtlessly felt like dumping lies on you. You see, that English teacher did not teach God's grammar lesson. His grammar lesson is, "Don't put a period where I have put a comma, because I have a plan for every life I create."

In Jeremiah 29:11, God tells us he has plans for us—good plans. And while maybe the hurtful words don't go away so easily, healing can happen in the heart and mind of a woman when she begins to let go of lies to embrace God's truth. Many times the biggest battles we women fight are the lies we believe and speak about ourselves. And as hard as it is to fight those lies, it is even harder to watch our daughters and granddaughters walk in the same lies we do. The reality is, the world offers no truth. If we don't learn to walk in God's truth, we will leave a legacy of lies for our own children to battle.

Many of us have experienced *spiritual identity theft*. We've lost our confidence in who we are in Christ, and we feel worthless or wounded by someone's words.

Others of us hold in our hearts a false identity. We believe a lie about ourselves, and that lie defines us.

You do not have to let others' hurtful words define you anymore. Those who spoke them did not give their lives, as Jesus did, to prove your worth.

TODAY'S BIBLE LIFE COACHING

You will know the truth, and the truth will set you free.

JOHN 8:32

Jesus promises us that the truth will set us free. Where can we find this kind of truth? How can we get our birthright back from the one who has stolen it from us? I don't know who broke your heart or struck you with lies, but I do know how to reverse the curse and help you walk in the truth your soul is craving.

In John 10:10 God warns us that Satan wants only to kill, steal, and destroy us. The best way for Satan to accomplish his mission is to give us a false identity. Jesus gave His life to give you a new identity—the kind of identity that is carved so deeply on our hearts that it can never be erased by another person's hurtful words.

Embracing our Christ-given identity can only happen if you trade truth for lies. You need to renew your mind by speaking, reading, and believing who you are in Christ. I have learned that if we don't know our true identity, then we are vulnerable to allowing someone else to give us a false identity. If we are not submerged in God's truth, we will become victims of spiritual identity theft.

No one can define you without your permission. If you continue giving the people around you power to tell you who you are, then you are no longer a victim of spiritual identity theft—you are a volunteer.

I would love to help you with your truth makeover. So first let me pray for you:

I pray in Jesus' name that you find the truth of who you are in Christ. I pray that you will have to stop looking to a man or other women to define your worth. I pray that you will begin to crave God's Word more than man's words of affirmation. May you find the truth you're longing for and the key to unlock and release the lies inside of your soul.

Here's how to go about your truth makeover:

Speak the truth. Whenever a lie is spoken to you or enters your mind, speak this phrase to yourself out loud: "That is a lie. The truth is . . ." Then say the truth out loud so your mind will hear your mouth. For example, if someone speaks a hurtful word to you, then speak to yourself out loud: "That is a lie. The truth is, my worth is not in what anyone else says about me. I will not allow someone's hurtful words to define me any longer."

Fast off lies. Try a seven-day fast by not speaking anything negative about yourself or repeating any lies that have been spoken over you or about you. If possible, ask a friend to hold you accountable to speak only truth.

Read the truth. Read these Scriptures that speak to the truth, which is that you are

  – chosen by God (1 Pet. 2:9)
  – a new creation (2 Cor. 5:17)
  – holy and pure (Eph. 1:4)
  – a trophy of His grace (Eph. 2:8)
  – His Princess Warrior (2 Tim. 4:7)
  – His beloved bride (Ps. 45:11)

Write the truth. Take one of the Scriptures above that speaks to your heart and write it down, personalizing it with your name. Put it in a beautiful frame and place it somewhere you can see it.

His Princess Love Letter

I believe if your heavenly Father wrote you a personal love letter for today, it would read like this:

Beloved Princess . . .

You are royalty even when you don't feel like a princess. How you feel about yourself will never change the truth of who you are in Me. You are My treasure, and I have chosen you. If you ever begin to doubt your significance, just look to the cross and remember I gave My life to prove your worth. I see your heart and I know you fight to find truth. So start by recognizing who I am: the King of Kings and Lord of Lords—and your Daddy in heaven. Saturate yourself in My truth and you will discover how loved and treasured you are.

Love,
  Your Lord who is Truth

TODAY'S *T*REASURE OF TRUTH

You are the Lord's treasured Princess, and how you feel about yourself will never change who you are in Christ.

3

FIGHT TO BE SET APART

> You have been set apart as holy to the LORD your
> God, and he has chosen you from all the nations of
> the earth to be his own special treasure.
>
> DEUTERONOMY 14:2

Let's define what it means to be set apart. If you look
up the phrase *set apart* in the World English Dictionary,
it is defined this way: to keep something for a specific
use or purpose.

If you look again at the above Scripture from Deuteronomy, you will see it is a chosen position that God
has set you apart for.

When I first became a Christian at age twenty-four, I
felt pressure to be like every other Christian. It quickly
became frustrating to try to model someone else's life
in Christ, because God designed each one of us differently. My good intentions to be like my other Christian

sisters left me feeling like I would never measure up. There were only two things I did well—talk and make people laugh. I did not realize that my obsession to talk to any poor soul within five feet of my reach could make me set apart. However, I have learned to use my endless words for God's glory, and not just to be heard. I have discovered that God actually gifted me to help others find joy as they laugh at life and that my gift of joy can encourage hurting hearts.

Today I still have to fight to find my confidence in Christ, but I am free to be myself. I am more confident than ever that it is not what we do that sets us apart—it is how much we allow the Holy Spirit to live through us that truly sets us apart.

Set apart can also mean to live differently than the world lives so God's character can be seen through you. It is not to become a "Christian clone" with no originality. Bold Paul was set apart to be a prophet, shepherd boy David was set apart to be a king, teenager Mary was set apart to give birth to the Son of God, fisherman Peter was set apart to be an apostle. What all of these people have in common is that none of them tried to be set apart in their own strength, but when God called them, they answered the call. They let God set them apart at any cost—even if it meant being rejected or alone. Real freedom comes when you crave being set apart for God's purpose more than wanting to squeeze into a man-made mold.

TODAY'S BIBLE LIFE COACHING

You can be sure of this:

The LORD set apart the godly for himself.
The LORD will answer when I call to him.

PSALM 4:3

I want you to be sure of this, my sister Princess: you are set apart, chosen by God to stand out for His glory. It is time for you to get comfortable in your royal wardrobe and embrace who you are in Christ. If you think about it, why should you waste your days trying to fit in with the world, and miss your chance to stand out and make a difference by the way you live and the way you love?

It's time to become more concerned about your witness and your walk with God. Let Him help you finish the work you were sent here to do.

Take a moment to write or text yourself three things you can change about your life. Let these be things that will set you apart and set you on the path of your God-given purpose.

His Princess Love Letter

I believe if your heavenly Father wrote you a personal love letter for today, it would read like this:

Beloved Princess . . .

I have called you to be set apart, just as I called those who came before you. I know this calling will sometimes come with great cost, but the eternal rewards are priceless and beyond comparison. Just as I did with Queen Esther, I have given you the ability to walk in such a way that all will see you are divinely Mine. Some will admire you for your dedication to Me. Some will want you to fail rather than follow your lead. You may fall because you are not perfect, but your mistakes can be the tutors that make you wiser. Don't put pressure on yourself to be perfect. I'm the only one who can perfect you, My Princess. All I ask is that you let Me set you apart, so that I can use you as a witness for the world to see.

Love,

 Your King who sets you apart

I knew you before I formed you in
your mother's womb.
Before you were born I set you apart
and appointed you as my
spokesman to the world.

JEREMIAH 1:5 NLT[2]

TODAY'S *TREASURE* OF TRUTH

It is not our perfection that sets us apart . . .
It is His perfection that stands out in our lives.

4

FIGHT TO KEEP YOUR FAITH

When your faith is tested, your endurance has a chance to grow. So let it grow, for when your endurance is fully developed, you will be perfect and complete, needing nothing.

JAMES 1:3–4

Won't it be nice when we get to heaven and can see the face of our heavenly Father—and then we won't need our faith to believe? I think one of the hardest questions for any Christian to answer when a tragedy occurs is, "Where was God when that happened?" Even Jesus had a moment on the cross when He cried out these words to His Father in heaven: "Father, why have You forsaken Me?"

I am not going to try to defend God or to claim to you that following Jesus takes away the pain and problems in this life. What I want to talk about is how to keep your faith when it feels like God has forsaken you. There will be times that you will have to fight to keep your faith in the midst of your pain.

I remember when I took a step of faith to witness to my Jewish grandma on her deathbed. She was the woman who best showed me a mother's love when I was growing up, so I desperately wanted my Jewish grandma in heaven with me. I remember walking into the room when she was just a few days from death. I lay down next to her with tears in my eyes and whispered, "Grandma, I want you to go to heaven, and Jesus made the way for you to get there."

I was sure that my faith could save my grandma, but to my surprise she turned her frail body away from me and asked me not to come to her funeral. I was a new Christian at the time, and when I took this first step of faith, it seemed that God had forsaken me. Not only did I lose the only mother figure I knew, I lost my Jewish family. I had to fight to keep my faith. I felt disappointed in God, and my faith was fractured.

Today my battle for my Jewish family is over—all my Jewish family members are born-again Christians. As excited as I am that my Jewish family knows the Lord, I am also very aware that not all battles appear to have a happy ending. What I have learned about life's battles is that when the anger, disappointment, and pain have all finally lifted, somehow we find ourselves more compassionate and more like Jesus. Life can be very hard at times, but pain can become the key that opens the door to our destiny if we allow it to birth a passion inside of us.

In my ten-year faith fight for my Jewish family, I discovered that surrendering those I love to God gives me perfect peace. When God was all I had, I discovered God is all I need! Even when you don't "feel" Him, He is holding your life in His hands. He fights for you when you are in the midst of a personal battle. He carries you when you are too weary to walk on your own. He will part your sea of hopelessness and reassure you of His faithfulness once again.

TODAY'S BIBLE LIFE COACHING

In 1 Samuel 23:16, Jonathan went to find David and encouraged him to stay strong in his faith in God. Let me be a spiritual mom to you right now and offer some words of wisdom. First of all, when your faith is feeling fractured, the last thing I want you to do is talk to a discourager. Instead I encourage you to do the following three things to protect your heart to refuel your faith:

1. Don't share personal battles with people who bring you down, because their negativity will fracture your faith even more.
2. Don't give up your faith because of how you feel in the middle of a battle; God is glorified best when there appears to be no hope . . . He brings new and powerful hope!
3. Stay in church even when you're mad at God. It truly is where you need to be when in battle. To keep the faith, you need to surround yourself in God's truth.

His Princess Love Letter

I believe if your heavenly Father wrote you a personal love letter for today, it would read like this:

Beloved Princess . . .

It's time to surrender your fears, your insecurities, your pain, and even your loved ones completely to Me. I want your whole heart and mind and soul to be worry-free. I want your complete trust so you can focus on your faith and be free of the spirit of fear controlling you. Give up the fight of trying to figure it all out. Don't let your circumstances hold your heart hostage or cause you to lose your confidence in Me. I am asking you on this day to answer this one question: In whom do you place your trust?

Love,
  Your trustworthy King

So do not throw away this confident trust in the Lord. Remember the great reward it brings you! Patient endurance is what you need now, so that you will continue to do God's will. Then you will receive all that he has promised.

HEBREWS 10:35–36

TODAY'S *TREASURE OF TRUTH*

Faith battles can birth great things inside of us and give our hearts a deeper and more passionate relationship with God.

5

FIGHT THE TEMPTATION TO QUIT

The godly may trip seven times, but they will get up again.

PROVERBS 24:16

When I was a little girl, my father was a Hollywood DJ. He also hosted beauty pageants, so I spent a lot of time watching girls walk down the runway doing that famous pageant wave.

Before I became a Christian, I had become addicted to watching beauty pageants. I dreamed of a day that I could walk down that glamorous runway and wave at everyone ever so gracefully.

That day finally became reality. I was going to be in my very first beauty pageant, and I worked very hard to prepare for it. Keep in mind I had just lost sixty pounds in preparation for the competition, and I was especially excited about the evening gown segment.

I was all dressed up in my gown and ready to walk down that glamorously lit runway. I did my little wave, smiled as big as I could, and gracefully strolled toward the judges. With my elegant gown, for the first time in my life I was feeling beautiful, until I came to the end of the runway—where I fell off the stage right onto the judges' table. Everyone in the audience gasped!

I was humiliated. And hurt. My hip felt dislocated, though fortunately it wasn't. But as I lay there flat on my face, fighting the temptation to quit, something rose up inside my soul that was bigger than my embarrassment. I still wanted to win! So I got off the judges' table, walked up the stairway that led up on that stage, and said to the room, "I just wanted to make sure you would remember me."

The audience rose to their feet and applauded wildly. Believe it or not, I did end up winning the crown of Miss San Jose that night. After the pageant the judges came up to me and said they did not have me picked as a winner, but they changed their vote because of the way I reacted to my fall.

I didn't know the Lord when I was in that pageant, but I know Him now. I took quite a fall that night, and

I have taken other falls since that very embarrassing moment. We all fall down, or sometimes life pushes us down. Many times our foundation has been so shaken that we feel like we are in a freefall and can't find solid ground to stand back up.

The truth inside the heart of every man and woman screams, "I want to *win*." No one wants to lose in life. We just don't know how to recover from the fall. Sometimes we hide like Eve in the Garden, sometimes we run away like Jonah, and other times we hide like Gideon. But God is so faithful and so there for us that He will find us in our weakest moment when we want to quit and lovingly lift us back up again.

Just because you feel like quitting does not mean life is over. Failure is never final with God. Sometimes a fall gives us an encounter with grace as we allow the Lord to lift us up from our painful place of humiliation. Sometimes our falls hurt both others and ourselves. But every time I've thought, *I can't get up again*, and have cried out to my King, He has always heard me, and He has always stretched out His hand to help me stand and continue serving Him.

The reason I tell you about my Miss San Jose Pageant is because I learned a very important life lesson from that night. I learned that it is not only how we act that makes a difference in our lives; it is also how we choose to react to pain, disappointment, and rejection. These reactions can determine whether we win or lose in this life.

Keep in mind that there is not a soul on this earth who won't experience failure, disappointment, and discouragement. Our beloved King David had to get up from the shame of neglecting his duty to be on the battlefield and committing adultery. The apostle Peter had to get up from the guilt of denying Jesus three times after bragging he loved the Lord more than everyone else. Do not misunderstand me—there is a price to pay when we fall and sin against God. However, the same God who disciplines us because He loves us also sent us a Savior to give us the power to get up and finish our faith fight.

Don't let anyone tell you God cannot redeem whatever you have done. You were born again to win victory in every area of your life! Ask the Lord to help you get up, and let Him handle whoever and whatever is keeping you down—and you'll win.

TODAY'S BIBLE LIFE COACHING

Get up and go to the great city of Nineveh, and deliver the message I have given you.

JONAH 3:2

Jonah wanted to quit before he even started. But God raised him up, even though Jonah had run from God's will for his life. I love it that when we want to quit and we don't feel like living for God, our Father in heaven believes in us even when we do not believe in ourselves. It may take a storm or two before we finally call out to Him to pick us up and put us in the center of His will, but He will not let us stay down. He knows how hard it is to get up when you fall down or when others put you down. Today He tenderly says to you, "Even if you fall seven times, My Princess, I will always help you back up again!"

One of the greatest battles we fight every day is the one in our mind. Our flesh tells us to quit trying to live for God. It screams the message that we will never be good enough, and that is a lie. Too many times we allow our failures to define us.

So let me take the pressure off you. Absolutely no one in the Bible or in history who did something great to further God's Kingdom lived a perfect life. Each hero of the faith loved the Lord and, despite their failures, never quit. This is the key to their success in serving the Lord. They answered His call on their lives despite their failures, despite difficult circumstances, and despite people who hurt them or discouraged them.

Our King loves us no matter how many times we fall. In fact, He is always there to pick us up, heal our hearts, and help us start walking again.

His Princess Love Letter

I believe if your heavenly Father wrote you a personal love letter for today, it would read like this:

Beloved Princess . . .

I know many days you feel like a weary warrior, too tired to fight. I see you when you have exhausted your faith and lost your passion for My people. Today I want to paint an eternal picture for My beloved warrior. Every act of kindness you share will water someone's thirsty soul. Every time you pray for someone, you are changing their destiny from darkness to light. You are more than a light in the darkness. Your faith will continue to be a raging fire that will burn in the hearts of many generations who follow your works on earth.

Love,
  Your eternal King

TODAY'S *TREASURE* OF TRUTH

God is *not* looking for perfection when you do His work on earth. Instead, He is looking for your heart commitment to Him.

6

FIGHT FOR EACH OTHER

You know very well what trouble we are in. Jerusalem lies in ruins, and its gates have been destroyed by fire. Let us rebuild the wall of Jerusalem and end this disgrace!

NEHEMIAH 2:17

I love the way Nehemiah handled the disgrace of God's people. Sure, he was brokenhearted, and the truth is that Jerusalem's gates had been destroyed, but his heart wanted to rebuild and put an end to the disgrace.

Today too many of our relationships lie in ruins. Hearts are broken, friendships are fractured, families are divided. We feel destroyed and alone. We can do one of two things. Either we can keep talking about the destruction of our relationships and replay the pain over and over again, or we can choose to pray, pick up

God's tools, and start rebuilding what is broken and disgraced. That's what Nehemiah did.

Relationships will continue to be a battle if we don't know how to fight for each other. Coming from my dysfunctional family, I witnessed many nights of fighting each other. I realize today that they really wanted to fight *for* each other but did not know how.

We all want to love and be loved, so let's learn to fight for each other and, as Nehemiah says, "end this disgrace."

TODAY'S BIBLE LIFE COACHING

For we are not fighting against flesh-and-blood enemies, but against evil rulers and authorities of the unseen world, against mighty powers in this dark world.

EPHESIANS 6:12

Our relational battles can only be won when they are fought in the spiritual realm first. Fight on your knees for those you love. Pray hard, because the greatest battle you may be fighting is the one inside your own heart, and blame and bitterness will not rebuild anything.

Many of us have never been taught how to handle our own hearts, let alone anyone else's. Many of us live with a constant internal fight. We beat ourselves up with guilt and regret for all the things we should have done and all the things we shouldn't have said.

Maybe you've been deeply hurt, and the only relief you can find is causing others pain so you don't have to deal with yours.

Maybe you're the victim of abuse where someone has done unjust and horrible things to you.

If this is you, the first thing my mother's heart wants to do is hug you and say I am so sorry if you have been a victim.

These feelings are very real, and I don't want to be insensitive. But whoever was cruel to you cannot keep you from God's plan for your life or His healing love. I want to help you be free to love and to receive love. Later in this book we will learn more about how to handle those feelings, but for now I want to talk to you about how to fight for those you love:

Pray for wisdom. God promises if we pray for wisdom, He will give it to us. Don't waste your time rebuilding without the right tools. Pray, seek godly counsel, and look to the Word to learn how to love.

Pray for yourself. What does peace in a relationship look like? See Romans, where we're told, "If it is possible, as far as it depends on you, live at peace with everyone" (12:18 NIV). So how do we handle the impossible people God acknowledges in this Scripture? Where do we start to rebuild when our hearts have been broken and it appears the relationship is destroyed and beyond repair?

If I learn to love the way God wants me to love, I must allow Him to examine my heart first. Then I must do whatever I can do to bring peace to the conflict. Believe me, it is not easy to do when you are in the heat of a relational battle. The last place we want to look is inward when someone has wronged us. So look upward and pray and ask God to show you what you can do to bring peace to the relationship

Pray for impossible people. God knows those people in your lives, which is why He says "if it is possible." If you are beating yourself up because you can't get a breakthrough in an impossible relationship, then it may be time to stop fighting and leave the impossible in God's hands. Paul and Barnabas did this when they parted ways. They just couldn't work out their disagreements. Even though they walked away from their relationship, God still used each of them to multiply His ministry. They ministered through their lives separately, instead of together.

Sometimes our biggest internal struggle is to let go and let God take over our relationships.

Pray for His will. Sometimes we fight so hard for what we want out of our relationships, we forget to ask God what His will is in our relationships. Being a mother, I dreaded the day it was God's will for me to let go of my son and let him grow into a man. Today I love the man my son has become and thank God He gave me the strength to let Jake go and grow.

If we are holding on too tightly, it will be hard to find God's will for any of our relationships. I know it seems scary to surrender our relationships to God, but actually there is complete freedom when you let go of the need to control others and grab on to your Father's hands in heaven.

Fight your differences. Proverbs 27:17 tells us, "As iron sharpens iron, so a friend sharpens a friend." We are all wired to think and see things differently. God wants to use our differences to sharpen us. Don't waste your relationships fighting to get someone to see your side. Fight to understand how the other person is wired and what you can learn from him or her about yourself.

Fight to resolve the conflict. We're told in Matthew 18:15, "If another believer sins against you, go privately and point out the offense." This is huge when it comes to protecting your relationships. Too many times when we are angry with our girlfriends or husband, we tell everyone besides the person we are mad at. To conquer conflict we have to do it God's way.

Jesus gives us two specific instructions in this verse. Go privately and talk to the person directly. Too many times we tell everyone but the one who offended us how upset we are, and that will not rebuild the relationship. It will ruin the relationship if we do not handle conflict God's way. Secondly, if someone offends you, pray and then go talk to them in love. Don't ignore offenses against you, or it will affect your relationships. But do make sure you come in love. You may want to start by saying, "I know you did not mean to hurt me, but . . ."

Let me offer a prayer for you:

I pray in Jesus' name, may you fight the tempta-tion to engage in relational battles that drain your strength, trying to prove your point or win your way or defend yourself. I pray you let your Lord be your defense. I pray you will never again get caught in the trap of blame and bitterness. May our God give you the wisdom to know what to fight for, for those you love, and how to fight in a way that brings blessings and breakthroughs to all of your relationships. In Jesus' name, Amen.

His Princess Love Letter

I believe if your heavenly Father wrote you a per-sonal love letter for today, it would read like this:

Beloved Princess . . .
    I know how hard it is for you to feel content in your home when you're always wanting one more

thing to make it the perfect place. I long to give you beautiful things that turn a house into the haven of a home; but My Princess, you must first learn to let Me build in you a place of peace and contentment. Do your best to rest in Me and wait for Me, and then I will give you what I know will benefit you the most. I want you to make your home a place that builds relationships and reflects who you are in Me. Remember that your loved ones need you more than any material thing. So decorate your home with joy, fill it with timeless memories, and create a safe place to grow up in Me.

Love,
  Your King and your Resting Place

Peace I leave with you; my peace I give you. I do not give as the world gives. Do not let your hearts be troubled.

JOHN 14:27 NIV

TODAY'S *T*REASURE OF TRUTH

Love is not a game to win. It is a gift worth fighting for.

7

RUN TO GOD

The name of the LORD is a strong fortress;
the godly run to him and are safe.

PROVERBS 18:10

Where do you run when life overwhelms you, and you cannot take any more? Maybe you're feeling overwhelmed by your circumstances, or maybe life has hit you harder than you ever expected. I know many times life does not seem fair or just. I wish I could give you a reason for every sad and awful thing that happens on this earth. I wish I could pray away all the pain this life brings. What I do know is that our Lord feels our pain and hears our prayers and has the power to help us overcome anything in this life.

Before I became a Christian, when I was in pain, I ran to food, drugs, and alcohol to escape, and as you know, it caused destruction in my life. Eventually, however, I believed I was destined for more than destruction. I wanted desperately to crawl out of this deep, dark hole of despair, but the harder I tried, the deeper I fell. I had nowhere to run.

Even after I became a Christian, I did not know how to process the pain this life brings. Somehow, I thought that following Jesus would eliminate emotional pain. So whenever I experienced emotions that did not feel godly, I ignored them. I thought if I kept my feelings covered up, they would go away. I handled my heart the same way I did before I was a Christian. I put my life in fast-forward by setting more goals and filling my schedule with excessive busyness. I did this so I would not have to feel or deal with anything emotionally difficult.

In theory, that sounds like it might work, but in real life it causes emotional meltdowns. At one point in my life, I had buried so much of my emotional pain that every part of my body was hurting. I had panic attacks, crying spells, loss of memory, and chronic depression. When I had no more strength or desire to run any longer, I finally found freedom and powerful peace. I learned to run to God and cry out to my Daddy in heaven.

I don't know where your heart is at this moment, but I do know how to lead you to your Father in heaven, in whose presence healing begins and strength is renewed so you can run free in Christ.

TODAY'S BIBLE LIFE COACHING

Hezekiah received the letter from the messengers and read it. Then he went up to the temple of the LORD and spread it out before the LORD. And Hezekiah prayed to the LORD.

2 KINGS 19:14–15 NIV

I don't know where you have been running when you're hurting, but I do know your Daddy in heaven is lovingly waiting for you to run into His arms. Sometimes, however, we don't feel God's comfort when we run to Him. Why? Because we run away from His presence too fast for Him to have a chance to reveal Himself.

Let's do the following three things today:

1. Pray and ask God to show you the areas of your life that you are holding back from Him.
2. Write a list of hurts you want to tell your heavenly Father.

3. Be still after you do the above and trust Him to comfort you.

His Princess Love Letter

I believe if your heavenly Father wrote you a personal love letter for today, it would read like this:

Beloved Princess . . .

You are destined to win. I know how tired you often become, running everywhere except to Me. If you want to win this endurance race, you must let go of living your life without Me to guide you. You'll find that My grace will lighten your step, and My favor will follow you when you draw close to Me. No one can comfort you like I can. In those times when you will stumble and fall while you run to Me, I will pick you up. I will do this as many times as it takes, and I never grow tired of picking up My beloved girl. Make it your daily passion to run to Me and with Me, and I will carry you over the finish line of your faith. Together we will win!

Love,

 Your Father who comforts you

Remember that in a race everyone runs, but only one person gets the prize. You also must run in such a way that you will win.

1 CORINTHIANS 9:24 NLT[2]

TODAY'S _TREASURE_ OF TRUTH

When you are too weak to run the race, allow God to carry you to the finish line.

8

RUN TO HIM
WHEN HURTING

The LORD hears his people when they call to him for
help. He rescues them from all their troubles

PSALM 34:17

I know how hard it is to believe we truly can run to an
invisible God, a faceless Father, and cry out to Him,
believing He hears our cry. But the truth is, God becomes visible to us as we take a step of faith toward
Him when we are hurting. We find Him in a very real
way when we become desperate for Him to rescue us
from the troubles of this world.

Daniel found Him in the lion's den. Moses found
Him in front of a sea of hopelessness. Joseph saw God
move him from a prison to a palace. Running to an
invisible God makes Him become more real than ever.

The arms of heaven are always open to you!

TODAY'S BIBLE LIFE COACHING

In my distress I cried out to the LORD . . .
He heard me from his sanctuary;
  my cry to him reached his ears.

PSALM 18:6

Many times I find myself fighting back tears when I am in pain. It is like I am afraid to release those painful places tucked in my heart. I hide them from God and hope they will just go away. My heart struggles to let my soul be cleansed with tears. Yet the truth is, crying out to God is like a spa for your soul. He tells us in His Word, "Those who sow in tears will reap with songs of joy" (Ps. 126:5 NIV). We will find the freedom we are looking for when we surrender our heartache to heaven, and allow our heavenly Father to handle our heart.

Pain is still a part of my life, as it is for everyone. The key to a heart at peace is not dodging or denying pain; it is learning where to run with your heavy heart. It is allowing God to enter into those dark places that only His light can heal.

If you are hurting right now, I want to encourage you to let go of your tears, and let your Lord wash away the pain with His holy presence. He longs to run to you and give you comfort when you cry out to Him. He is a compassionate God, and He is waiting to heal your hurting heart.

His Princess Love Letter

I believe if your heavenly Father wrote you a personal love letter for today, it would read like this:

Beloved Princess . . .

When you hurt, I hurt with you. I too walked through this world with a broken heart. Don't hold back—instead call out My name. In your dark hours, I will carry you into My presence where true healing begins and love you back to life again. I am your Lord and the lover of your soul, and I want to be the shoulder your tears fall on. I promise, My Princess, your tears will not be wasted when they are poured out to Me.

Love,

Your Prince Jesus who will wipe away your tears

Those who sow in tears will reap with songs of joy.

PSALM 126:5 NIV

TODAY'S *TREASURE* OF TRUTH

Your Lord feels your heavy heart. You are His beloved bride, and He wants you to take a break from the worries of this world and rest in His arms today.

9

RUN TO HIM WHEN ANGRY

"In your anger do not sin": Do not let the sun go down while you are still angry.

EPHESIANS 4:26 NIV

Have you ever been told "Emotions are ungodly," or "Ignore your feelings and live by faith"? Do you wonder why, then, did God give you emotions in the first place, if you are supposed to ignore them? Perhaps you have asked yourself, "If God loves me, why am I feeling such pain?"

Let me assure you God designs emotions for a reason. God designed you to feel, because you are created in His image. The almighty God has feelings too. Did you know there are more than two thousand instances in the Bible that refer to the emotions of God?

Emotions, both positive and negative, were created by God to reveal the condition of the human spirit.

Sometimes they are warning signs that indicate something is wrong inside us. Just as physical pain reveals that there is something wrong with our body, our emotions can be a warning signal that something needs attention in our spirit. Ephesians 4:26 says, "Be angry, and do not sin" (NKJV). The sin isn't in feeling angry. However, the anger leads to destruction if we don't know how to deal with it.

TODAY'S BIBLE LIFE COACHING

I had a dad who expressed a lot of outward anger and a mom who had severe inward anger called depression. Because of this, I only knew two ways to process anger—either yell and scream or shut down and hold it in. Neither of those options will bring freedom, so I want to help you break free from any anger and bitterness controlling your heart.

> *Write out your anger.* I have found that writing my feelings on paper helps me process them, and even more so if I write it to God. Take time today, if you are dealing with anger, to write a letter to your Daddy in heaven who cares deeply about the

things that hurt you. You're His girl and He is your God. He wants you to hand Him your anger and broken heart. Give Him your heart and He will replace the pain with peace and give you the grace to get through even the hardest of times.

Confess anger to God. I know a lot of anger can be justified, but confessing your anger will keep you clean and create a right heart in you. It may sound strange to talk to a holy God when you feel angry, bitter, jealous, resentful, or hateful. But there is only one way to break free from the anger controlling you, and that is to confess it to God every time you find yourself feeling angry.

The truth is, we cannot hide from Him, and He loves us no matter what emotions we are feeling. If we keep trying to handle our own anger, we are playing God. But if we surrender to our loving Lord, He will replace our anger pains with His perfect peace.

Allow me to take you through a prayer of confession below. Read it and make it your own.

Dear God,

I confess my anger to You right now, and I invite You into those dark areas of my heart where I have hidden my anger. I give You permission to enter in

and shine light. Please shine Your light on my sin.
Please show me how to live free from the anger
that is controlling me. I choose to believe You are
cleaning me now and creating in me a new heart.
Father, I believe You are giving me the supernatural
strength to walk in the Spirit and not in my flesh.
In Jesus' name I pray, Amen.

Don't breed more anger. When my husband and I
were struggling in our relationship several years
ago, I made the mistake of telling my children
and girlfriends how angry I was at him. Of
course, all I birthed by doing that was even more
anger and bitterness. I got my friends angry, and
worse yet, I got our children upset. Clearly, I let
my anger control my behavior.

Today I know that crying out to God and confessing my anger is my only way to find freedom from
anger controlling me. Too many times we tell everybody about our anger—everybody but God. The more
people we tell, the more bitter we become. Instead, let
the healing words lift the stone of anger off your heart.

Before I let go of this issue of anger, I have to talk
about anger with God. Where do you run if you are

mad at God? This is a huge issue, because when something horrific happens or a life crisis has fractured your faith, what do you do when you are angry at the only One who has the power to heal your heart and comfort you?

It is impossible to find everlasting relief when you're mad at God. Sadly we live in a fallen land, not a fairy tale. Pain is a part of this life because of the sin of man, not God. Knowing that, however, does not lessen the pain of losing a child, of a husband having an affair, of the loss of a job, or the betrayal of a trusted friend. The list is endless of unjust things that break our hearts and make us angry.

First, I want to reassure you that your heavenly Father has the ability to understand when you are mad at Him, and He will never stop loving you or finding ways to prove to you He is there in the midst of your pain and anger. Your Lord Jesus knows what it is like to feel like your heavenly Father has forsaken you. When Jesus was on the cross, there was a moment when He cried out to God, asking why His Father had forsaken Him. He cried out in the garden the night He was betrayed. In His suffering, He asked His Father for another way—a less painful way.

Yet Jesus trusted His Father God's plan. He knew the ultimate victory was at the cross. Don't ever doubt that God is with you. If you will cry out to Him in prayer and give Him your anger and the crushing weight of your circumstances, He will walk with you through the garden of grief and straight to the cross—where your trials will be transformed into triumph and renewed passion for life.

If you are angry at God, don't hold it in. I encourage you to cry out to Him in your anger and confess that anger. Ask Him to comfort you even when you are mad at Him.

His Princess Love Letter

I believe if your heavenly Father wrote you a personal love letter for today, it would read like this:

Beloved Princess . . .

I know there is much happening in the world to get angry about. But anger is a trap set by the enemy of your soul. If you take the bait of anger, you will become bitter, and nothing good is ever birthed out of bitterness, My beloved. So when you feel angry, cry out to Me and confess that anger. I am the One who can handle your heart and walk you through the battlefields of rage and anger. I will teach you how to live a life free from the destruction anger brings. You can be at peace as you learn to trust Me and to deal with all those who have hurt My girl.

Love,
  Your King who is just

Dear friends, never take revenge. Leave that to the righteous anger of God. For the Scriptures say, "'I will take revenge; I will pay them back,' says the LORD.*"*

ROMANS 12:19

TODAY'S *TREASURE* OF TRUTH

Many times painful places put us on the path we are destined to travel and bring us closer to the heart of God.

10

RUN TO HIM
WITH YOUR NEEDS

I will answer them before they even call to me.
   While they are still talking about their needs,
   I will go ahead and answer their prayers!
                    ISAIAH 65:24

Many of us have lost our homes or our jobs, and in the process, we have lost our faith that God takes care of our needs. It appears to us that no matter how much we pray, He will not give us the things we have asked Him for.

I want to reassure you that, like a loving Father, God knows what is best for His girl. Our faith struggle is not because God does not meet our needs; it is because we forget who our Father is. He is God, and He knows our true needs before we even ask.

The inspiration for this book came as a result of one of the darkest hours of my life when I lost everything I thought I needed to feel secure. God reached down and took away all the material things that I believed I needed to build my happy life.

At one time, my husband and I owned a production company, where we showcased models and actors similar to an *American Idol* type of show with agents and directors from Hollywood. It was an amazing opportunity to share Christ with Hollywood. We sincerely honored God in our business. For many years He met all our needs with this company and even more than we needed.

But in one particular city where we were working, there was an agency that began slandering our company. The people at this agency did not like the fact that we were Christians working in their marketplace. This greatly affected our company's success. We began to fall into debt and could not meet our financial needs. We prayed and asked God to save us from the financial crisis we saw coming, but that did not happen. We lost our home, our company, and our ability to pay our bills.

Now you might be thinking what I was: Why did God not protect us? Why did He not meet our needs and save our home? There were many days when I lifted prayers of disappointment before the Lord.

The strange thing is, though, at the same time God was taking things away, He was opening different doors. One of those doors was to compete in the Mrs. United States Pageant. This opened up because our production company could no longer keep our commitment to produce an Arizona state pageant. In the end, that company insisted I stand in for my state for the telecast.

Now let's get real for a moment! I felt like I was losing everything. During this stressful time, I miscarried three babies and gained twenty pounds from stress-eating. All that to say, I certainly was not thinking, "I know! I'll just be in a beauty pageant. That will fix everything!"

As you know, I ended up winning the national crown, and it was that crown that sent the media after me. They found my before-life-in-Christ photo when I was sixty pounds overweight and addicted to drugs. The media blasted my past all over the world.

Let's talk girl-talk for a moment. You know as well as I do, when you don't feel good about your life and your body, and you believe the lie that God has forsaken you, the last thing you want is to be in the public eye.

I am not trying to get your sympathy. I want you to see how God meets your needs according to His will and not ours. I have found we see His mighty hand at work much better when the distractions we think we need are removed. When this life is over, we won't care what we wore or where we lived. The only thing that will matter is that we have all we need to further His Kingdom on earth.

TODAY'S BIBLE LIFE COACHING

So don't worry about these things, saying, "What will we eat? What will we drink? What will we wear?" These things dominate the thoughts of unbelievers, but your heavenly Father already knows all your needs. Seek the kingdom of God above all else, and live righteously, and he will give you everything you need.

MATTHEW 6:31–33

As I've said before, I did not have a secure home life throughout my childhood. I came out of it believing that I wanted a perfect home in perfect order with a white picket fence where I could be happy. This was my greatest need from my perspective. This would bring me peace.

And I needed a husband who always adored me so I would feel secure. I needed wonderful children who always obeyed so I could enjoy being a mother. Oh, let's not forget the cuddly dog that would not poop in the yard so I would never step in it or have to clean it up, but instead would use the toilet. Okay, I'm going overboard, but I do have a point—and that is, we need to go to God and pray the following:

- Dear God, what do I need to draw closer to You?
- Dear God, what do I need to be more like You?
- Dear God, what do I need to keep me from getting so comfortable that I forget to rely on You?
- Dear God, what do I need so I can meet the needs of others?
- Dear God, what do I need to step into Your purpose for my life?

Such prayers can change our hearts and position us to experience a far greater life than we could ever give ourselves. I suggest praying the following prayer too:

Dear Heavenly Father,
Please forgive me for all the times I took Your place
in my life by trying to meet my own needs. Right
now, I place my future in Your loving hands. I am

ready to come before Your throne and trust You
no matter what. Today I trade all my fears for a re-
newed faith in You. Today I know in my heart that
You will provide more than I ask for. May I never
doubt You again!
In Jesus' name, Amen.

This same God who takes care of me will supply all
your needs from his glorious riches, which have been
given to us in Christ Jesus.

PHILIPPIANS 4:19

His Princess Love Letter

I believe if your heavenly Father wrote you a personal love letter for today, it would read like this:

Beloved Princess . . .

Walk in My confidence. I know the world whispers
in your ear that what you possess defines who you
are, and what you look like determines your worth.
This is a lie, My love. The generations to come will
never remember you for the things you accumulate or
the efforts you placed in your appearance. In fact, the
harder you strive to collect more things and to perfect

your image, the more insecure you will be about who you are and why you are here. I am in you and you are in Me. I will give you all you need. Now go and walk through your world in the confidence that I've uniquely equipped you with all you need to impact the lives of those around you forever!

Love,
  Your King and your Confidence

> *For the LORD will be your confidence*
> *and will keep your foot from being caught.*
>   PROVERBS 3:26 NASB

TODAY'S *TREASURE* OF TRUTH

Our God is not our puppet master. He is our Master, and He will provide all we need to complete His master plan for our lives.

11

RUN TO HIM
WHEN TEMPTED

> The temptations in your life are no different from what others experience. And God is faithful. He will not allow the temptation to be more than you can stand. When you are tempted, he will show you a way out so that you can endure.
>
> 1 Corinthians 10:13

Many times we feel alone in our struggles with temptation. To make matters worse, we beat ourselves up about it. I want to offer a word of truth, according to the Word of God: We all battle temptation, large or small, and we need God to make a way out of that temptation.

For the first seven years of our marriage, Steve and I appeared to be the perfect match. I love his family. We both love the Lord and attended church together.

We enjoy eating healthy and exercising. We love being in ministry, and we love being parents.

But the hidden truth was that during our first seven years as husband and wife, I often felt more alone than when I was single. I spent much of those first seven years only pretending to be happy and fighting the temptation to walk away.

Even though I knew Steve loved me, I didn't feel close to him. It may have been because the pain from my parents' divorce resurrected itself in my marriage. Whatever the reason, I was fighting temptation and did not know I could run to God with that temptation.

Finally, one night I broke down and told Steve what I was fighting with, but he had no idea how to help me, so he ignored my cry. After a while, I grew tired of my pit of despair and wanted a cure for my loneliness. I was paralyzed by my pain and weakness. Needless to say, this left our marriage wide-open for the enemy's trap.

Eventually, temptation knocked at the door of my heart in the form of another man—a friend whom Steve and I had led to the Lord. This man spoke the kind of words that opened the door of my heart. He broke down walls I had been hiding behind. I could share my deepest feelings and biggest dreams with him. He showed me a love that I longed for, and I almost convinced myself it was God's will for me to leave my husband. I almost gave up all I cherished—my marriage, my ministry, and my dreams.

Even though we never had a physical affair, we had an emotional affair—an affair of the heart. I knew it was a sin, but I could not stop; I was caught in the trap of temptation.

Finally I cried out to God, and He used my husband to rescue me. Steve discovered my hidden affair of the heart, but to my complete astonishment, he did not condemn me. Instead, he did something amazing: he came to me with tears in his eyes and roses in his hands and said, "This is my fault for not showing you how much I love you and making you feel safe and accepted."

Steve's expression of love that day did more than rescue me. It made him my hero, and it saved our marriage. I am more in love with my husband now than ever. His extraordinary expression of love that day put me back where I really wanted to be all along: in his arms.

I want to be a spiritual momma to you right now and warn you that whatever temptation you're battling with, don't hide it from your Father who loves you. Don't keep your temptation to yourself. Bring it out into the light where freedom rules over darkness.

TODAY'S BIBLE LIFE COACHING

David was able to overcome the temptation to kill King Saul when he had the chance. But let's look at a weaker David and talk about a very real and heartfelt prayer he cried out to God. It's found in Psalm 109:8, where David boldly asked that Saul's days be few and that God would replace him with a different king. This was David's eloquent way of saying, "Please let Saul go away somewhere in the wilderness and die!"

If you read any of David's psalms, you will see there was nothing artificial about David's relationship with the Lord. He didn't hide his rage, his fears, his disappointments, his worries, his praise, or his love from his heavenly Father. The only thing David did hide was the temptation he battled with when he saw beautiful Bathsheba bathing naked.

Maybe David did not run to God because he felt such a strong pull of the flesh to have this woman that he wanted her more than he wanted God to give him a way out. Or maybe he thought he could handle being tempted in his own strength. Maybe he deceived himself into believing he loved God so much he would never fall. David only fell when he stopped fighting his inward battle with temptation.

Let me encourage you to get free from the stronghold of temptation by drawing closer to God. We need our Lord to make a way out for us, give us the strength to walk through the exit door, and slam it shut.

His Princess Love Letter

I believe if your heavenly Father wrote you a personal love letter for today, it would read like this:

Beloved Princess . . .

Don't be afraid to run to Me when you feel tempted. I know everything about you already, My love. You will need Me to show you the way around. I love when you come to Me and share your feelings, your failings, and your fears so that I can more fully reveal My power to you. Temptation is not a game, and you will have to run as far from it as you can to keep from falling prey to it. Call to Me when you feel weak, and I will always make a way of escape for you. I won't force you to follow Me out of harm's way. You ultimately will make the choice to run to Me.

Love,
 Your King, the Great Escape

You are tempted in the same way that everyone else is tempted. But God can be trusted not to let you be tempted too much, and he will show you how to escape from your temptations.

1 CORINTHIANS 10:13 CEV

TODAY'S *T*REASURE OF TRUTH

Inward battles don't mean you're weak—they mean you're a warrior fighting to do what is right.

12

RUN TO HIM
WITH BLINDERS ON

It bursts forth like a radiant bridegroom after his
wedding.
It rejoices like a great athlete eager to run the race.

PSALM 19:5

When I was a little girl, my dad would take me to the
racetrack. The horses mesmerized me. They were fast,
they were focused, and they were determined to finish
their race a winner. But what amazed me even more
is that they ran their race with blinders on. This meant
they could only see forward. They could not see who
they were running next to. They could not see who
was watching from the audience. They could not even
see the jockey riding them. They could feel the jockey,
though, guiding them with every stride. The horses
somehow knew the jockey could see what they could

not. In other words, they trusted their jockey to get them to the finish line.

Our God is our jockey, and we don't need to see or feel anything but His Spirit leading us. It does not matter who is cheering us on or putting us down. All we need to do to finish our life race as a soul winner is to put our blinders on so that we look straight ahead and then allow the living God inside us to help us win people for Christ. If you think about it, what good will it do if we run for the praises of people and conquer nothing for the Kingdom of God?

TODAY'S BIBLE LIFE COACHING

I was blinded by the intense light and had to be led by the hand to Damascus by my companions.

ACTS 22:11

God had to literally blind the apostle Paul to help him step into his destiny.

King David may have never stepped into his destiny if he did not have blinders on. It was David's blinders that kept him from seeing the size of Goliath the giant and the look of fear on everyone else's faces.

His blinders did not change the fact that the giant was bigger and stronger than David.

The giant had the reputation of being unbeatable, and it appeared David was defeated before he even stepped out on the battlefield. Even in light of this, David did not see that giant as too big to hit—he saw him as too big to miss. David's blinders gave birth to his destiny.

When we make up our minds to run with blinders, we won't lose sight of the eternal prize. Blinders are a good thing, if we are running our race for God's glory and not our own.

If you are feeling like everyone around you is better, smarter, stronger, and faster, it is because you don't have your blinders on. You are in the same race as your Christian brothers and sisters, and your race is equally as important as theirs is to furthering God's Kingdom. When you feel like you're losing your race, I want to encourage you not to look at what you see in the world but instead to focus on what you know to be true in the Word.

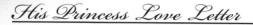

His Princess Love Letter

I believe if your heavenly Father wrote you a personal love letter for today, it would read like this:

Beloved Princess . . .

There will be times when you will feel I am far from you, but this is not true, My love. Your feelings will deceive you, but I never will. I am the Truth that will forever help you find your way back to Me. So whenever you feel lost, look up so I can light your way. When your world seems dark, I will be your compass and your comfort. I will carry you over the finish line of your faith when you're too weary to run. You will never be lost as long as you keep your eyes on Me. Even when you don't have the strength to go on, I will be your strength.

Love,
 Your Prince

You go before me and follow me.
You place your hand of blessing on my head.
Such knowledge is too wonderful for me,
too great for me to understand!

Psalm 139:5–6

TODAY'S *T*REASURE OF TRUTH

Your Father sees perfectly what you cannot. He will remove any obstacle in the way of His will for you.

13

ELIMINATE MIND INVASION

Do not be conformed to this world, but be transformed
by the renewing of your mind.

ROMANS 12:2 NKJV

I have had the privilege of meeting people from all
walks of life. I've met people with fame and fortune;
people who are lost and lonely; people who are intel-
lectual, interesting, and intriguing; people who are
powerful; and people who are beautiful. But no matter
where I have walked in life, I have found a common
goal existing in every heart. Everyone is searching for
purpose and peace of mind. Our souls and hearts long
for internal peace.

That peace can't be found in beauty magazines or
on the television screen or in a bigger house or better
income. If we are not careful, we will allow the enemy

to steal our peace and our purpose by what we watch and read and listen to.

If you're tired of your mind messing with your heart, and you want to break free from fear, confusion, and negativity, then let's look at the root cause.

Freedom in Christ is free, but living it out comes with a cost—the cost of giving up the things that destroy our minds, our morals, and our message of faith.

It's not that our God doesn't want His daughters to have any fun or entertainment. He wants to protect our minds, our bodies, and our souls from destruction. If you don't believe this is true, take a good look at the fearful, negative, and depressed people who have traded their God-given life purpose for a moment's pleasure. Chasing temporary satisfaction outside of the loving boundaries of God's protection leaves us vulnerable to embracing the enemy's deception and empty promises. The enemy wants nothing more than to distract God's princesses from their calling.

TODAY'S BIBLE LIFE COACHING

*But there is another power within me that is at war
with my mind. This power makes me a slave to the
sin that is still within me.*

ROMANS 7:23

If a police officer came to your door and warned you
that your neighbors had just been robbed and killed,
you would be on the lookout for anything that could
let that enemy into your home or near your loved ones.
Our King warns us in His Word that there is an enemy
after us who is out to kill, steal, and destroy (see John
10:10). He also warns us that if we are not careful, we
will help him (the devil) accomplish his mission by
what we read, watch, and listen to. We will let him destroy our values, our minds, and our children through
the modern entertainment we allow in our homes.

Here is some direction in eliminating mind invasion.

Consider this Scripture:
   *Fix your thoughts on what is true, and honor-
   able, and right, and pure, and lovely, and admi-
   rable. Think about things that are excellent and
   worthy of praise.*

PHILIPPIANS 4:8

Ask yourself: How do you feel about the world you live in after watching hours of bad news? How do you feel about the way God created you after reading a beauty magazine? Is the entertainment value worth trading for time with God and those you love?

Go on a media fast: Try fasting off all TV and beauty magazines for the next week and see if your mind begins to think more clearly and if your spirit has more peace. You may see the world around you in a whole new light.

Pray:

Dear Lord,

Please show me what I am reading and watching that is keeping me from You. Help me see what I am allowing into my home and my heart for what it is—and then give me the courage and conviction to say no to what I shouldn't be allowing. Grant me the self-discipline to give up whatever You ask me to surrender, and starting today, to read and watch that which will build my faith and character. I pray in faith that You will transform me and cleanse me from the inside out.

In Jesus' name I pray, Amen.

His Princess Love Letter

I believe if your heavenly Father wrote you a personal love letter for today, it would read like this:

Beloved Princess . . .

In your weakness, I will keep you strong, My child. I am well aware of the many things in this life that war against your spirit and your soul. I know it feels like distractions and difficulties are sent daily to test your character and convictions. Remember, My love, this life is not a dress rehearsal. It's the real thing, and I'm training you through these tests to trust Me. I am preparing you today for your future life in heaven. So seek Me in prayer for My strength, and don't give in to temptation or compromise. They are like quicksand in your path to righteousness. Hold on to Me and My power within you, and I promise that you will make it through. When wicked winds try to extinguish the flame of your faith or try to cause you to compromise, stand on My truth . . . I am your solid Rock, and you can conquer anything in My strength.

Love,
  Your King and your Rock

*Temptations that come into your life are no different
from what others experience. And God is faithful. He
will keep the temptation from becoming so strong that
you can't stand up against it. When you are tempted,
he will show you a way out so that you will not give
in to it.*

1 CORINTHIANS 10:13 NLT[2]

TODAY'S *TREASURE* OF TRUTH

Watch your thoughts . . . they become your words.
Watch your words . . . they become your actions.
Watch your actions . . . they become your habits.
Watch your habits . . . they become your character.
Watch your character . . . it becomes your legacy.

14

ELIMINATE
DISCONTENTMENT

After all, we brought nothing with us when we came
into the world, and we can't take anything with us
when we leave it. So if we have enough food and cloth-
ing, let us be content.

1 Timothy 6:7–8

This Scripture is a great reminder that the stuff we
think we need to have in order to be content will not
be going with us when we go home to heaven.

And discontentment is not just about wanting stuff.
Most women are not looking for more stuff to feel
content. They are looking for a different life. We battle
more with discontentment when we think about how
our lives turned out.

Do you find yourself thinking things like:

"If I had her husband, I'd be happy too."

"If I had her body, I'd be confident too."

"If I had her job, I would feel successful too."

Maybe those thoughts are even true, but what do they breed? They breed discontentment, and we find ourselves never settling into our own lives because we keep wanting to live someone else's. This kind of discontentment can't be fixed by buying something. It can only be fixed by surrendering it to God.

I wasted several years of my life telling myself, "I will be happy when . . ." and when I got where I thought I needed to be, it was never what I thought it would be. It always left me wanting more. Can you relate?

If we keep dreaming about what we don't have, we will never find contentment with what we do have.

It's time to check in to our own life and become content!

TODAY'S BIBLE LIFE COACHING

Not that I was ever in need, for I have learned how to be content with whatever I have.

PHILIPPIANS 4:11

How do we learn to be content wherever we are? I understand that this is easier said than done. We have to fight the temptation to look at what others have and keep focused on what is in front of us so we can live for today. Let me give you a few things that can help free us from discontentment:

Speak with gratitude: Our words are a powerful weapon. If we talk about things we are discontented about, then we will think about them even more, which leads to us becoming miserable. The key is to speak out loud every day the things you are thankful for.

My friend Lisa shares this story of how the orphans she adopted experienced a breakthrough to their freedom. Every day in the worst circumstances you can imagine in a third world country, these boys decided to sing praises of thanks for who God is and for their home in heaven. I believe those praises birthed a choir of forty-five African boys who came to America to raise money for that orphanage. Not only did they raise money in less than six months, all forty-five were adopted into loving American families. I share this to say if you cannot think of any blessing on earth, lift your voice and your eyes to the heavens and watch what happens to your heart. You will find the contentment you are longing for!

Remember the power of prayer: May I suggest praying this prayer?

> *Dear Lord,*
> *I confess I have battled with discontentment.*
> *I have been fighting for more and forgetting to*
> *give what I have to glorify You in my life. Please,*
> *God, turn my discontentment into praise. I pray*
> *You would lift the veil off my eyes that I might*
> *see my life through heaven's eyes and walk the*
> *rest of my days looking up at You. Today I let*
> *go of the discontentment in my heart. Today I*
> *give You whatever I have to further Your King-*
> *dom on earth. Amen.*

Embrace today: Ask God to open your eyes to the blessings of this day. Don't miss today by thinking about tomorrow. Live today as if it is your last day, and in the process, you will embrace it!

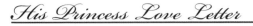

His Princess Love Letter

I believe if your heavenly Father wrote you a personal love letter for today, it would read like this:

Beloved Princess . . .

   I love you and I don't want you to waste your walk with Me wanting more of this world. Crave more of Me and you will find what you're looking for. Capture this day and you will see My presence all around you. I will send a breeze to whisper I am near and a sunset to kiss you good night. Let Me wrap My love around you like a blanket on a cool evening and you will feel Me close. Let this day be the day you embrace your life!

Love,
  Your King and your Eternal Beauty

> *Charm can be deceiving*
> *and beauty fades away,*
> *but a woman who honors the* LORD
> *deserves to be praised.*
>   PROVERBS 31:30 CEV

TODAY'S *T*REASURE OF TRUTH

Contentment comes when we decide to be where we are and give what we have for His glory, not for our happiness.

15

ELIMINATE
APPROVAL ADDICTION

Am I now trying to win the approval of men, or of
God? Or am I trying to please men? If I were still trying to please men, I would not be a servant of Christ.

GALATIANS 1:10 NIV

When I was an overweight teenager, the homecoming
king at school called me "Sheri the Whale." I was so
hurt and embarrassed I made up my mind I would
prove my worth by losing weight and therefore capture the approval of my peers. I was convinced that if
I were thin and pretty, I would get the approval I so
desperately wanted.

What I discovered is that losing weight, buying new
clothes, and winning a beauty title were not enough to
make me feel good about myself. Somehow it didn't
feel the way I dreamed it would. As a matter of fact,

I began to live for the words of praise about my new look. It felt good when I was getting attention, but I could never seem to get enough (kind of like chocolate). I became obsessed with doing whatever I had to do to get one more compliment. No amount of praise could eliminate my approval addiction.

Now I know I am talking about high school, but what about when we become adult women? Is there a magical age at which we feel free from needing the approval of others? I have seen very few women of God who do not fight daily for the approval of others. Maybe we're not as obvious about our approval addiction as we were in high school, but we do some crazy things as adult women to find our worth. If you think about it, it is the approval of man that keeps us from living for God—the one who preapproved us even before we were born. We need only to look to our Maker for acceptance.

TODAY'S BIBLE LIFE COACHING

Ask yourself these questions:

Whose approval am I seeking? Am I living my life for the approval of God or the praises of people?

It's time to pray for release from approval addiction. I know that when I'm fighting approval addiction, I have to cry out to God for help. We all desire approval, but when we give that desire to God in prayer, it weakens the power the need for approval has over us.

Speak out loud statements like these:

"My Daddy in heaven adores me."

"Thank You for proving my worth, Jesus, by Your sacrifice on the cross."

"His love is enough for me."

The truth is, we will exhaust ourselves by performing for a world that does not want to praise us. When we choose to live for God's approval, we find freedom from others controlling our confidence.

His Princess Love Letter

I believe if your heavenly Father wrote you a personal love letter for today, it would read like this:

Beloved Princess . . .

I know you want to be accepted by others. But I did not create you to find your worth in this world. I don't want you to waste another day desperate for approval of others. Their praises will never be enough, and they cannot compare to My adoration for you. Live for My approval and you will be free to be confident in who you are to Me. You are My beloved daughter and the apple of My eye.

Love,

 Your Father who gladly accepts you

TODAY'S $\mathcal{T}$REASURE OF TRUTH

What others think of you does not define your worth. They did not give their life to prove your value.

16

ELIMINATE CHAINS

I will walk in freedom,
for I have devoted myself to your commandments.
PSALM 119:45 NLT²

Do you sometimes feel like you're in chains? Many of us carry virtual chains of pain and bitterness. And those chains are very real and very heavy. But sometimes these chains can almost feel like a covering of protection. Sometimes that need for protective covering comes from abuse and injustice.

This is hard for me to address, because the mother's heart inside me breaks every time a woman, man, or child has been abused or treated unjustly. I would love to have the power to come to you personally and wipe out your memory of every horrible thing you've had to witness or experience in this sinful world.

I am truly sorry for whatever you have been forced to walk through because of someone else's actions. I know how heavy chains of rejection and abuse can feel—I've felt plenty of that myself.

My prayer for you right now is that you will find the faith to trust God and forgive those who have hurt you. When you forgive, you can unlock your life and be free, once and for all.

TODAY'S BIBLE LIFE COACHING

Therefore, if anyone is in Christ, he is a new creation; the old has gone, the new has come! All this is from God, who reconciled us to himself through Christ and gave us the ministry of reconciliation.

2 CORINTHIANS 5:17–18 NIV

In the Old Testament, Joseph had a great call of God on his life. But when he was young, his brothers tried to paralyze him from his purpose by abusing him and selling him into slavery. And if that was not enough, later on he was falsely accused of rape and thrown into prison.

But with God's strength, Joseph was able to leave the chains of blame and bitterness in his Father's hands and complete the call God had on his life.

Joseph knew his brothers had had nothing but hateful, evil intentions for him when he lived with the family. When he saw them years later, he didn't deny that they had hurt him deeply. But Joseph knew God had a plan for him, and he wasn't about to let anything destroy it, including his brothers.

Just as God was with Joseph through his abuse and imprisonment, He is with you and He will lift you up and unlock your chains. You will witness how He turns what was intended for evil into good.

There is a power stronger than those who have hurt you, and that power is from God. He can—and He will—unlock your chains if you will lift your hands to heaven and cry out to Him. Our Lord is knocking at the door of your heart, asking you to let Him set you free. I encourage you today to let Him deal with those who have made you feel like you're in prison. He is a just God and will not tolerate those who attack and abuse His own.

His Princess Love Letter

I believe if your heavenly Father wrote you a personal love letter for today, it would read like this:

Beloved Princess . . .

I know there are those who commit what seems like unforgivable sin. Sometimes such a person has hurt you. But I am a just God, and I will deal with those who have hurt My daughter. I want to set you free from this deep, dark pain inside your soul, so I am asking you to unlock the prison door that holds your heart hostage from receiving My blessings. If you refuse to forgive, you are not only hurting those who have caused you pain, you are hurting yourself, My love. Now take the key to freedom I offer today and release yourself by releasing the person who caused you pain. It's time to be free.

Love,
  Your Father and Redeemer

TODAY'S *TREASURE* OF TRUTH

No one can cancel the call of God on your life.
You are His.

17

ELIMINATE FEAR

He will cover you with his feathers.
  He will shelter you with his wings.
  His faithful promises are your armor and
    protection.
Do not be afraid of the terrors of the night,
  nor the arrow that flies in the day.
Do not dread the disease that stalks in darkness,
  nor the disaster that strikes at midday.

PSALM 91:4–6

Let's talk about fear. And I would love to say that dealing with it is as simple as just praying the fear away or pretending evil does not exist.

But it is not that simple. When you are under fire, and fear captures your heart, you don't always feel the covering of His feathers, as is written in the Psalms. When we are under attack, we don't always feel protected.

Each of God's chosen ones has felt fear, and many allow that fear to affect their actions and reactions to life. God is not mad at us because we feel fear; no, He loves us and wants to hold us like a little girl and wipe away all our fears. He wants us to feel safe in His arms of love.

But how do we not feel fear when terrors happen day and night in the world we live in? How do we walk through the fire without feeling the fear of being burned up or burned out?

TODAY'S BIBLE LIFE COACHING

Psalm 112:7–8 tells us: "They do not fear bad news; they confidently trust the LORD to care for them. They are confident and fearless and can face their foes triumphantly." These verses remind us we don't have to fear bad news; however, it does not say we won't feel fear. If we were not going to battle with feelings of fear, God would not have felt the need to remind us hundreds of times in Scripture not to fear because He is near.

The truth is, we cannot eliminate what we feel when we face giants. But we can confess that fear to our Father in heaven and stop trying to be a woman of faith in our own strength. We can cry out to our Daddy in heaven when we are freaking out on the inside and let His powerful peace invade our fearful hearts. We can speak the Word out loud so fear loses its grip on our lives. We can eliminate the effects of fear by choosing to trust our God.

One of the things I like to tell my daughter when training her to be safe is this:

"We don't walk in fear, but we do walk in wisdom."

His Princess Love Letter

I believe if your heavenly Father wrote you a personal love letter for today, it would read like this:

Beloved Princess . . .

I have not given you the spirit of fear but of a sound mind. Therefore today I call you Fearless Princess, the way I called Gideon a valiant warrior when he was afraid to fight. I am the same God who gave Gideon the strength to win his battle with the enemy, and I am your God. The only time something will overtake your heart is if you take your eyes off Me. I don't want My girl bound in terror. As long as you are walking in My power and Truth, you have nothing to be afraid of. No matter what it looks like now, victory will always be yours. So fear not, My beloved. I will never leave your side, My Princess. Know that day and night I am fighting for you.

Love,
 Your Father in whom you can trust

TODAY'S *Treasure* OF TRUTH

Storms help remind us that God is the Captain of our lives. We have no need to fear.

18

EMBRACE LIFE'S BATTLES

When troubles come your way, consider it an opportunity for great joy. For you know that when your faith is tested, your endurance has a chance to grow. So let it grow, for when your endurance is fully developed, you will be perfect and complete, needing nothing.

JAMES 1:2–4

Most of us crave peace so much that we do anything to avoid walking through a battle. Don't get me wrong, peace is a gift from God, but the peace becomes most powerfully displayed on the battlefield. What I mean is, life will bring unexpected conflicts, and God will always deliver unexpected blessings from the hardship we walk through. We can embrace the battle, knowing it can birth in us a more intimate relationship with our heavenly Father and a better view of what really matters.

I know how hard it is to push through pain, but it is even harder to waste it . . . so let's embrace it and fight!

TODAY'S BIBLE LIFE COACHING

Cry Out . . .

Whether it's through painful tears like Jeremiah or loud songs of praise like Paul and Silas in a cold, dark prison, your crying out not only reaches the ears of a loving heavenly Father, it touches the souls of fellow prisoners and ultimately you as well.

Speak Out . . .

"God, I trust You are with me in this storm."

"God, I thank You for trusting me with this pain."

"God, You will not waste this pain. Please teach me more of You."

Take Courage . . .

Your single act of courage to hang on and praise Him through the storm will strengthen you and others around you. You may not even see it now, but one day—maybe tomorrow or perhaps in eternity—your moments of courage will be visible signposts that lead to great blessings and breakthroughs.

Dear Jesus,

I pray for my sister princess that You will use every tear she has cried to put a passion in her heart to do something great for Your Kingdom. Give her comfort in her dark hour and put a song of praise in her heart. Give her back her hope and remind her she will not remain in this painful place for long. Even now, I pray You draw her closer to You. May she never forget that she is Your precious jewel and that You will shake the earth if that is what it takes to see her chains fall to the ground. Amen.

His Princess Love Letter

I believe if your heavenly Father wrote you a personal love letter for today, it would read like this:

Beloved Princess . . .

Don't get discouraged, My beloved; pain is a part of life. But I promise you that I will turn every tear you've cried into joy, and I will use your deep pain for a divine purpose. Don't try to hide your hurts from Me. I know everything about you. You are Mine, My beloved! I'm the only One who can handle your heart, for I too have felt great pain, rejection, and anger. But we can go through every trial together. Hand in hand I will lead you back to My place of peace and joy after the storm. The sun will shine on you again, and your hope will be restored.

Love,
  Your Father who rescues you

TODAY'S *TREASURE* OF TRUTH

Battles are won on your knees before God. Don't try to fight when God is waiting for you to ask Him for help.

19

EMBRACE PRAISE

> Around midnight Paul and Silas were praying and
> singing hymns to God, and the other prisoners were
> listening. Suddenly, there was a massive earthquake,
> and the prison was shaken to its foundations. All the
> doors immediately flew open, and the chains of every
> prisoner fell off!
>
> ACTS 16:25–26

Paul understood the power of praising God in a painful, dark place. Prison is not just a place with iron
doors. Prison comes in many forms, one of them
being when our hearts seem locked up and we feel
totally paralyzed by pain. Many times we feel there
is no escape from the hurt our hearts feel. These are
real feelings, and the key to freedom is not to pretend
pain is not real. The key needed to unlock a hopeless
heart is praise.

What you may see as broken inside yourself, your Father sees as beautiful. He is the one who makes beautiful things out of broken hearts. He is the same God who took a brokenhearted orphan named Esther and turned her into a queen who saved her people. He loves you, and He will not waste a single tear you have shed. Your God can and will use whatever is broken in your heart for His glory. I know it's hard to believe, but His grace and mercy will shine brightest in those broken places. He will not only use what is broken, He will rebuild your life into something beautiful. Praise Him, and you will feel the chains fall off as your King turns your sorrow into joy and your pain into purpose.

TODAY'S BIBLE LIFE COACHING

God causes everything to work together for the good of those who love God and are called according to his purpose for them. For God knew his people in advance, and he chose them to become like his Son.

ROMANS 8:28–29

When we are in a dark hour, it's hard to believe that God works everything together for good. I don't ever want to minimize the pain this life brings. If I could go back and live my life my way with a loving family and a secure, safe home, of course I would—but that is not an option. So I have a choice: I can remain paralyzed by pain, guilt, anger, and disappointment; or I can choose to learn from the broken places in my life, look to the Lord for wisdom and direction, and be thankful for the broken places I have walked. Knowing that pain helped to develop and prepare me for the road I walk today in full-time ministry.

When it seems like there is no escape from sadness and your heart is overwhelmed, I encourage you to follow Paul's lead and begin praising God in a song. Play praise music all day in your home and in your car and sing even when nothing is playing.

I still have sad days, but I know what to do when I am in pain. I cry out to God, like we talked about earlier, and then as the tears begin to cleanse my soul, I begin to praise Him even when I don't feel like it.

I would love to pray for you if you are in a painful place right now:

Dear Jesus,
Help me remember that I am not alone when
battles come my way. Please give me Your peace
and Your power to persevere in this world. I choose
on this day to trust You and praise You through this
storm, because I know You are my Life Preserver.
Amen.

His Princess Love Letter

I believe if your heavenly Father wrote you a personal love letter for today, it would read like this:

Beloved Princess . . .

Do not be afraid, for I have ransomed you. I have called you by name. I will never leave you or forsake you, My love. I am your faithful Father, and you can trust Me. I am here with you when you go through deep waters of great trouble. Your human eyes may deceive you when you are in a test of your faith. But when you are in the fiery furnace of your faith, I will not let you burn up or burn out. You can confidently embrace any battle, My beloved, because you are My daughter. Victory is yours before you see it. So trust Me in any trial, and you will find peace and comfort.

Love,
  Your Daddy in heaven

TODAY'S *T*REASURE OF TRUTH

Praise is not denying the problem; it is pointing to God as the power.

20

EMBRACE BOUNDARIES

> Mark out a straight path for your feet;
>> stay on the safe path.
> Don't get sidetracked;
>> keep your feet from following evil.
> PROVERBS 4:26–27

Proverbs tell us to stay on the right path and not to get sidetracked. I don't know about you, but I feel like I lived most of my life sidetracked by people pleasing.

When I first became a Christian, I wanted to be a "Super Christian." I thought one of the best ways to be that superhero was to please everyone. As a Christian, I would never want to offend others by telling them no. I would sacrifice too much of my personal life and set no boundaries or limits in my efforts to please people.

My lack of boundaries burned me out. "Super Woman" turned into "Super Bitter Woman." I did not feel blessed for all of the effort I was putting into being everything to everybody. I felt used and abused, and it was my own fault.

Boundaries are designed by God to bring freedom to your life. Yes, there will be people who do not understand why you won't allow them to run your life. Friends and family could be those who invade your personal space. People who are close to you feel like they have a right to your life, and they invade these boundaries. However, you may have to set moral boundaries to protect yourself and your family to have times to deal with issues in your home.

Let's not forget the critic in the corner or the guilt monster across the table sent by your enemy to break you down. I am not saying boundaries will be easy to keep. But I am saying that you will be more effective in your faith and have more peace in your heart if you will value yourself enough to embrace the boundaries God designs for your life.

It may be a battle. But the blessing of being in control of what you will and won't do is amazing. I invite you today to treat yourself to some God-given boundaries. You will love the security it brings to you and your family, and you will find freedom when you don't let others invade the space that was created for you and God.

TODAY'S BIBLE LIFE COACHING

From one man he created all the nations through-out the whole earth. He decided beforehand when they should rise and fall, and he determined their boundaries.

ACTS 17:26

The first boundary God made was when He created Adam and Eve. He gave them everything any human could ever crave. There was one boundary line that God asked both of them not to cross. Unfortunately, they did cross that line and wiped out the perfect world God designed for them and us.

That is exactly how Satan works. He convinces us that boundaries are bad and keep us from living our life to the fullest. How many times in your life have you looked back and thought, "If I had just said no," or "If I had just put my guard up, this would never have happened." When I look back on my own life, I wish I had embraced personal convictions and those

God-given boundaries. We can't change the past, but we can build new walls of protection that honor God—starting today.

I want you to picture *boundaries* as a beautiful fence built around your loved ones and yourself. Then decide what and who you are going to allow into that precious and private place of protection.

Ask yourself the following questions:

- What television programs will we watch?
- What kind of music will fill the air in my home or car?
- How much time will I spend talking on the phone today and with whom will it be?
- Whom in my life have I allowed to be a personal space invader?

Pray about:

- Some areas of your life or loved ones' lives that feel unprotected or unvalued.
- Distractions that may have invaded a valuable time or witness for the Lord.
- Turning off your phone and computer and tuning into your loved ones after 7:00 p.m. This

boundary will allow you to focus on the needs of your family.

And finally, write out some boundaries you believe should be set up this week. Here's how you might pray to get started on this:

Dear Lord,
I want You to invade my personal space. My life
is Yours, and I want to live it under Your umbrella
of protection. Please show me any boundaries You
want me to set, and give me the strength and wis-
dom to keep them. Father, I know You love me, and
I will trust Your lead. Amen.

His Princess Love Letter

I believe if your heavenly Father wrote you a personal love letter for today, it would read like this:

Beloved Daughter . . .
I'm your Father in heaven and I want you to protect your heart and your mind as you walk with Me. Don't allow others to cross over or break down the borders I have set to protect you. Embrace the boundaries and hold tightly to what

I have given you—a sound mind, a pure heart, and an abundant life destined to be lived for Me alone!

Love,

Your King and your Captain of courage

TODAY'S *T*REASURE OF TRUTH

Boundaries become your guide, your gauge, and your guard for life!

21

EMBRACE YOUR WEAKNESSES

[Jesus] said, "My grace is all you need. My power works best in weakness." So now I am glad to boast about my weaknesses, so that the power of Christ can work through me.

2 CORINTHIANS 12:9

I have dyslexia. I used to wonder why God would call me to write books but give me a learning disorder. I may be the only author who has written more books than I have read. I only type ten words a minute. There have been many moments I wanted to quit doing what I am called to do because of my weaknesses. But grace is the power to do something bigger than you could ever do on your own.

Maybe God entrusted me with a learning disorder because He has anointed me to write scriptural love letters in His voice. I like to joke that maybe He wanted a blonde like me with no thoughts of my own so I would not get in His way!

To be honest, I find great comfort in hearing about all the weaknesses of His chosen ones in the Word, especially in the apostle Paul's writing in 2 Corinthians 12:9. I love that Paul was highly educated, smart in every way, yet even Paul found his weaknesses and then talked about God working through his weaknesses, not his strengths.

I am not saying I don't value education, because I do. I am also not in any way putting myself up on a pedestal with Paul. I simply want to talk heart to heart with you. I want to be a spiritual mother and challenge you with hard questions.

How long are you going to put yourself down for what you are not, and when are you going to grab hold of who Christ is in you? When will you get out of God's way so He can do something great through you?

I wasted most of my life trying to build my confidence with what I accomplished or how I looked. Although we may have good intentions, our goal is to feel good about ourselves. Eventually that confidence fades and we find ourselves needing something more to feel good again.

It's a wonderful feeling to get a new job, a new haircut, or a new outfit—these things can make us feel confident on the surface. It is great to have goals and to accomplish them. But what have we accomplished if we forget who God is in us?

The only way to conquer our insecurities is to allow God to become all we need to feel secure. Let's embrace our weaknesses, knowing that He is strong where we are weak and that He shows His power through us *when* we learn to embrace our weaknesses.

TODAY'S BIBLE LIFE COACHING

The only way to build a confidence that will last is to trade self-defeating confidence with "God confidence." In other words, let's find our confidence in who we are in Christ, then use our God-given gifts and talents to do something to further His Kingdom on earth. As Scripture tells us, "I can do all things through Christ, who strengthens me" (Phil. 4:13).

When you look at your life through heaven's eyes and draw your strength and confidence from your God, you will be ready and able to face any giant that tries to kill your confidence. You will be able to step out in the battlefield of life and know that your God is with you and that He is your confidence and your power. In doing this, you will find the key to unlock the door to your destiny. And you'll pass that God-confidence on to your children.

Anytime you feel defeated because of your weaknesses, say out loud to yourself, "He is God and I am not. I can do all things through Christ who gives me the strength." Remember this Scripture:

> *The LORD is my light and my salvation*
> *—so why should I be afraid?*
> *The LORD protects me from danger*
> *—so why should I tremble?*

> PSALM 27:1

Let me pray for you, my friend:

In the precious name of Jesus, I pray you will embrace your weaknesses and become confident in Christ alone. I pray that God alone will define your purpose. May the realities of heaven become your foremost motivator—not the things of earth. I pray that as you draw your confidence from Him, He will use you to accomplish effective and everlasting things for His Kingdom. In His name, Amen.

His Princess Love Letter

I believe if your heavenly Father wrote you a personal love letter for today, it would read like this:

Beloved Princess . . .

Come to Me and tell Me what you're afraid of. Is it the future? Your health? Your circumstances? Your finances? Your security? Don't you know that I am Creator and King of all? I own all the resources in the universe. Nothing is beyond My knowledge or My power. Remember that I am your God and Salvation. I will never give you more than you can handle. Ask Me, in faith, about anything. Obey what I tell you to do, and you will feel your fear vanish. I am the Lord your God, and I delight in caring for you, My child. So do not fear, My Princess. I am always near.

Love,

  Your King and your fearless Leader

TODAY'S *TREASURE* OF TRUTH

Sometimes our God disables us to enable us. We can do more in His strength than we could ever do on our own.

22

EMBRACE BEING STILL

Be still before the LORD and wait patiently for him.

PSALM 37:7 NIV

I can remember many years of committing to anything and everything that was asked of me—and on top of that list of commitments was my own personal unrealistic list. Being still was never on my list. I was raised with a father who was a mover and motivator. Being still was looked at as lazy in my driven Jewish family. Because I did not know how to be still, I lived every day overstressed and overcommitted.

Being still is not something many of us have mastered. We feel like we have too much to do to stop and spend time with God. Even those of us in ministry can become so focused on what we want to conquer for God, we forget to go to God and get refreshed.

We underestimate the power of being still in His presence. To be honest, even while I was writing this book, I found myself missing my quiet time with God to meet my book deadline. I felt like someone unplugged my personal battery, yet I kept pushing myself to finish writing. One afternoon while I was writing, I ran out of wisdom to share. I cried out to God, "Why are You not giving me the words for this freedom book?"

At that moment, I noticed my iPod on the kitchen counter getting recharged. Maybe God wanted to use something as simple as my iPod to remind me to lie down and let Him recharge me.

At that very moment, I made a decision that I would not write a single word without my quiet time with God, and He gave me the breakthrough I was longing for.

Maybe it sounds silly to compare my iPod with my need to be still. But don't we recharge our phones, our computers, our electric toothbrushes? If we did not, they would not function. We women are in desperate need of recharging. It's time to stop running around and start running into our Daddy in heaven's arms so He can hold us long enough in His presence to give us the peace and quiet our soul is longing for.

Don't feel guilty for taking your time with God. Sometimes we need to shut off everything to hear His voice. Always remember the Scripture "Be still, and know that I am God!" (Ps. 46:10).

TODAY'S BIBLE LIFE COACHING

Do you ever wish you could put your life on pause and just catch your breath? I truly believe the cry of every woman's heart is to be still, but we don't know how to stop being busy. Our soul longs for a moment of silence. I think that is why spas and yoga classes have become so popular; we women are so desperate for a moment of stillness that we are willing to pay for it.

God desires us to be balanced, not burned out. I love spas, but let me give you some creative ways to quiet your spirit and be still:

- Lie down and listen to your favorite worship songs and soak in His presence.
- Lock yourself in the bathroom, take a bath, and pray.

- Turn off your phone and computer for twenty minutes a day and be in the presence of our God.

- Ask God to quiet your spirit and help you to be still. Remember, Scripture says, "My sheep listen to my voice; I know them, and they follow me" (John 10:27 NIV).

His Princess Love Letter

I believe if your heavenly Father wrote you a personal love letter for today, it would read like this:

Beloved Princess . . .

I long to be closer to you. I'm never too busy for you, My beloved. If you will turn off the things around you that drown Me out of your daily life, you will begin to hear Me in your spirit. When you don't know where to go, you will hear Me give you divine direction. When you are in need of a friend, you will hear Me whisper, "I am here." When you need comfort, you will hear Me call to you, "Come to Me." Don't let your agenda distract you from time with Me. Quiet your spirit. Know that I am your heavenly Father and you are My precious daughter—and I love when you crave time to be still with Me.

Love,
 Your King and the Voice of heaven

TODAY'S *TREASURE* OF TRUTH

If the devil can't make us bad, his next trick is to make us busy.

23

EMBRACE TRUE BEAUTY

> Charm is deceptive, and beauty does not last;
> but a woman who fears the LORD will be greatly
> praised.
>
> PROVERBS 31:30 NLT[2]

Where can we find the true definition of beauty in a world that reminds us daily what we are not and what we must have to feel beautiful? I have never met a woman who feels pretty enough to stop trying to be more beautiful.

But what does it take to make us feel beautiful? Where does this craving come from, and will it really matter what we looked like when this life is over?

I had the privilege of knowing a true beauty. Her name was Rachael, and when she was thirteen, doctors told her that cancer would take her life within eight weeks. When I called to pray with her, she said,

"Would you pray that, before I die, I can share Jesus with my entire school?"

When I got off the phone, I cried. Rachael's dying wish, her heart's desire, was not for herself but for others. She had an eternal beauty even though her earthly body was fading away. Rachael was committed to representing her King and sharing His beauty—despite her circumstances.

The doctors gave Rachael eight weeks, but God gave Rachael three years, and on her sixteenth birthday, she announced, "I am ready to go home to be with the Lord. I have finished what He sent me here to do."

Rachael made a final request of her high school principal. She asked if the entire student body could attend her funeral, and God granted her favor with him. Her principal made buses available for anyone who wanted to attend Rachael's memorial service. I had the honor of being there, and the church was completely packed. I watched busloads of teens with a wide range of backgrounds get off those buses and enter the church.

Rachael left one final beauty mark as she had written a letter for her pastor to read at her service.

Dear friends,

Please do not be sad for me today, for I am in a place where there is no more sickness, no more death, and no more tears. I am in heaven, and my prayer for you is that I will see you here someday and we will share eternity. My Savior Jesus Christ has made a way for you to get here.

Love, Rachael

When the pastor finished reading Rachael's letter, he asked how many kids wanted to ask Jesus into their hearts. Hundreds of kids raised their hands toward heaven and gave their lives to our Lord.

Rachael's cancer had given her a unique beauty. She became a beautiful reminder of what really matters—she was a star that pointed people to heaven. She cared more about the eternal lives of others than her own earthly life coming to an end. Rachael may have lost her hair in cancer treatments, but she won souls for the Kingdom of God. Her pretty body may have become weak, but her faith was stronger than ever. Rachael's life reflected more true beauty when she was sick and without hair than when she was fashionable and beautiful to look at. This true beauty of God left a beauty mark that can't be bought in a store.

TODAY'S BIBLE LIFE COACHING

I invite you to take a moment to ask yourself, What beauty marks am I making on the lives of those I love? Make a list.

Consider this Scripture:

God has made everything beautiful for its own time. He has planted eternity in the human heart, but even so, people cannot see the whole scope of God's work from beginning to end.

ECCLESIASTES 3:11

It's our time to look up and allow God to make us into the beautiful women we long to be.

His Princess Love Letter

I believe if your heavenly Father wrote you a personal love letter for today, it would read like this:

Beloved Princess . . .

I know you don't see yourself the way I do. You compare yourself to beauty idols who will soon be forgotten. If you could see how beautiful you are in My eyes, then you would see that your eternal beauty is a breath of heaven! When I look at you, I see a treasure ready to be discovered, a princess ready to shine. I have given you the kind of beauty that is everlasting. I lined your lips to speak words of life; I have given you beautiful hands to reach out to your hurting friends. The beauty I created you to be is a reflection of Me. The beauty you possess will leave eternal beauty marks on the hearts of all who were loved by you.

Love,
   Your radiant King who loves His beautiful daughter

TODAY'S *TREASURE* OF TRUTH

The irresistible beauty of His Princess is

> *A Beautiful Heart* . . . that loves God and loves others
>
> *Beautiful Eyes* . . . that look for the best in others
>
> *Beautiful Lips* . . . that speak life and encouragement
>
> *Beautiful Feet* . . . that walk in God-confidence

Beautiful Hands . . . that reach out to those in need

A Beautiful Life . . . that will forever be treasured by those she loved

24

DO LOVE YOUR LORD

Jesus replied, "'Love the Lord your God with all your heart and with all your soul and with your entire mind.' This is the first and greatest commandment."

MATTHEW 22:37–38 NIV

Jesus is asking us, His bride, to surrender her heart to heaven and fall madly and totally in love with Him. He wants His bride to give up everything that would keep her from experiencing His love and surrender completely to a loving relationship with Him.

It is true that I conquered and accomplished much without a love life with the Lord; being raised Jewish, I never gave a thought to Jesus. He was the last place I would have looked for true love. But today I must say He is truly the Love of my life, and there is no way I could live without Him.

I remember the night I had my first encounter with His extraordinary love. It was in my darkest hour and I felt hopeless and desperate for someone to love me.

I should have been happy at the time. I had a good life from the world's point of view. I had lost fifty pounds, gotten off drugs, and become a health nut. I had money, success, beauty titles, boyfriends, nice clothes; I drove a nice car and had a calendar full of appointments for places to go and people to see. Yet I still felt desperate for love and cried myself to sleep at night. On the outside I looked like I had it all together, but on the inside I was falling apart. I felt empty, lost, and alone, even when I was in a crowd of people who loved me.

Weight loss could only change my body, it could *not* fill my heart; and money could only buy me things, it could *not* buy me peace of mind. Beauty crowns could get me praises of people, but their praise could not give me peace. Somehow I became so depressed in my quest for true love that I began to fight feelings of suicide.

One dark night I convinced myself I had nothing to live for, so I checked into a hotel room with every intention of ending my life with an overdose of sleeping pills.

Yet at that moment, I cried out to God as my last hope—He must have heard my cry, because for the first time in my life I did not feel alone. I actually felt God's holy presence with me. I felt loved and at peace. Even though I did not understand this new love life with the Lord, I discovered one desperate cry for love from the Lord gave me what I had been desperately searching for: love, joy, peace of mind, a purpose for living.

When I called out to God that night, He gave me the greatest crown of all. It was not a crown bestowed by man but the crown of life—of everlasting life—bestowed by asking Jesus into my heart. This was a love I could not see, yet I could feel. It felt like I kissed heaven.

TODAY'S BIBLE LIFE COACHING

Our Lord promises that if we will seek Him with all our heart, we *will* find Him. Maybe you have been a Christian a long time, but you have never really experienced His love the way He longs for you to, or maybe you don't feel you deserve His love.

The truth is, none of us deserve His love. But His strongest desire for us is that we embrace His love as if it were living water, because it is. Life becomes meaningless and faith becomes fruitless if we are not in love with Jesus.

I am not talking about salvation; salvation is not a feeling but rather an act of faith. I am talking about becoming like a giddy bride when she is on her honeymoon. I know there are those who will tell you not to be concerned if you don't feel in love with your Lord, but God created us to crave His love and feel His presence.

Remember the Scripture that says, "May I experience the love of Christ, though it is so great I will never fully understand it. May I be filled with the fullness of life and power that comes from God" (Eph. 3:19).

Let's find creative ways to feel love for and from our very real Prince who gave His life to prove how much He loves us.

His Princess Love Letter

I believe if your heavenly Father wrote you a personal love letter for today, it would read like this:

Beloved Princess . . .

You have captured My heart, My Princess. I will always love you. From the moment I dreamed you up, I loved and adored you. This love I have for you is ever-present and never-ending. My heartfelt desire is for you to walk through all your days knowing you are truly the love of My life. I never want you to feel you have to earn My affection; nothing you have said or done can or will ever change the way I feel about you. I have chosen you to be My precious bride. If you allow your soul to settle in to Me and become one with Me, you will never doubt that I am forever and always devoted to you.

Love,

Your Prince Jesus who won't stop loving you

TODAY'S *T*REASURE OF TRUTH

There is nothing you can do to stop Him from loving you.

25

DO LIFE GOD'S WAY

The instructions of the LORD are perfect,
reviving the soul.

PSALM 19:7

Our God knows that walking in integrity becomes a
real fight that takes place inside our soul when injustice is done to our loved ones or to us. It is painfully
hard when your heart is broken not to give in to the
temptation to conquer evil by responding with evil.

One of my favorite stories in the Bible is the scene
where David catches King Saul sleeping while on his
manhunt to kill David. There is a tempting moment
when David could have taken justice into his own hands
and could have killed Saul while he was sleeping.

Now let's get real, no one would have blamed David
for killing Saul—after all, the king was trying to kill
David first. We call that self-defense.

But David's decision to take the high road of integrity and let God fight for him gave David divine power and God's protection during this battle for his life.

We all know life is not fair, and it seems crazy that God would ask us to do the right thing when the whole world does the wrong thing and gets away with it.

Joseph had more right to become bitter and take revenge than anyone in the Bible. His jealous brothers sold him into slavery and told his daddy he was dead. But integrity set him apart from the other slaves, and he was given a great leadership position.

It looked all good until another battle came his way when his boss's wife wanted Joseph for herself. Because he was a man of integrity, Joseph rejected her advances. Now this time it looked like God did not bless Joseph's integrity, because the wife falsely accused Joseph of raping her and had him thrown into prison.

That horrible act of injustice looked like the end for Joseph. He had no one to defend him. But he made a hard choice to trust God and continue to walk in integrity. Joseph's integrity took him even higher this time—from prison to a palace. He became third in command of the whole kingdom. God not only lifted him up, but He gave him the extraordinary gift of interpreting dreams and the wisdom to save the kingdom's people from starving in a seven-year famine.

TODAY'S BIBLE LIFE COACHING

It is true—life can and will throw us a lot of curves. And many times you may question "Where is God in all of this?" I wish I was able to explain why some things happen on this earth. But as the Bible says in Isaiah 55:8–9, His thoughts are higher than our thoughts and His ways are higher than ours. The one thing I do know, according to the Word of God, is that we are in a spiritual war. When nothing else is left and the world has robbed you of everything, remember this: The only way to win a battle is to fight with integrity and to pray for your enemies so you don't become like them.

Scripture tells us:

Be an example to all believers in what you say, in the way you live, in your love, your faith, and your purity.

1 TIMOTHY 4:12

Consider Job—a man of God who lost his wealth, his health, and his family; yet he would not allow Satan to steal his integrity. God ultimately gave Job even more than he lost.

His Princess Love Letter

I believe if your heavenly Father wrote you a personal love letter for today, it would read like this:

Beloved Princess . . .

Choose to live for Me. I will bless you and your loved ones if you make that choice. Every tough time in which you obey Me will become a foundation of faith in your family. Your commitment to My call will carve character in the next generation. Every prayer you pray will become a blessing passed down. Your courage will continue to bring comfort to many during their difficult times. Trust in Me. I, your God, declare on this day that your children's children will be forever blessed, because you lived your life for an audience of one—Me!

Love,
  Your King who gives you life

TODAY'S *TREASURE* OF TRUTH

His way is the only way to the blessed life He longs to give His children.

26

OPERATE IN YOUR APPOINTED POSITION TO BE A HERO

The angel of the LORD appeared to him and said, "Mighty hero, the LORD is with you!"

JUDGES 6:12

When I first became a mother, I wanted my son to see for himself the hand of God moving in his life. So I began to pray with him when he was only two. Almost every day Jake and I kept our appointment with God. We would ask Him to use us to do His work that day, and I was so encouraged to see a little boy be so passionate for prayer.

When Jake turned thirteen, I prayed that God would help him understand the true joy of giving. At the time, we lived in a small town in central Oregon where there was no mall. One day Jake and I drove to Portland for a big shopping spree. We had saved our money all year for our big day at the mall. As I drove, I prayed with Jake for a divine appointment—and our God didn't waste any time answering that prayer.

We walked into the mall and Jake was immediately off to the computer store. As I followed behind him, I happened to notice a young teenage girl curled up on a bench, shaking. It was freezing outside and she did not appear to have a coat. I couldn't see her face, but I could tell that she was very cold and in emotional pain. My heart broke for her. I couldn't help myself; I wanted to do something to help, so I approached her and said, "Please let me pray for you."

To my surprise she totally mocked me by responding sarcastically, "*Whatever*"—to which I shot back, "I'm not leaving until I pray for you." She looked at me with anger in her eyes and said, "Go ahead and get it over with." Jake walked up to us just as I began to pray this prayer:

"Dear God, I don't know what this girl has been through, but You do, so please let her know You love her and that You can and will help her. Please show her today, somehow, that You see her broken heart and You can restore all she has lost. In Jesus' name I pray, amen."

This precious girl went from cold and distant to crying uncontrollably. Then she began to share her story through her tears. She had gotten pregnant, but her parents had wanted her to abort the baby. She wanted to keep the baby and marry her boyfriend, who was the father of the child. Her parents had kicked her out on the streets. She and her boyfriend kept the baby, slept under a bridge, and still went to high school. But because they were homeless, they had given the baby up for adoption.

The girl's boyfriend walked up while she was sharing their story, and my son said out loud, "Mom, it's time to shop."

I said, "Jake, did you hear their situation?"

He said, "Yes, that's why we need to spend our shopping money on them."

That day Jake took the young man and bought him clothes, a sleeping bag, new shoes, and a backpack. I took the girl and did the same. At the end of our time with them, we got to pray the greatest prayer of all—the prayer for salvation. Then our ministry cut a check to get them in an apartment and off the streets.

As Jake and I drove back home without any shopping bags in our car, Jake said to me, "Mom, that was the best day I have ever had!" At that moment I realized that Jake will never remember anything I bought him when he is old, but he will never forget the day God used his life as a gift to someone else.

We don't need money to build those kinds of price-less memories with our children. If anything, money distracts us from what is really valuable in this life. But acting according to our divine purpose, living in God's power, and seeing Him answer our prayers are three of life's greatest treasures. Those are not things we can buy for our children. They are part of a legacy we build inside of them by our own examples of praying with purpose and acting on God's leading.

TODAY'S BIBLE LIFE COACHING

There are many things we can do each day to be a hero in someone's life. That said, not everyone is yours to rescue, so I don't want you to burn yourself out trying to rescue those you were not called to rescue.

To be a true hero of the faith, we must come to the rescue of those God calls us to serve. Start each day with the following suggestions. Then submit it all in prayer.

1. Write your "to-do" list. Then pray over it and ask God if that is His list for you.

2. Never abandon those in your life who need you most in order to save those who can be rescued by another. To make certain you don't do this, ask your family each day, "How can I be a blessing to you today?" This speaks loudly and goes deep into the heart of those you love. It keeps you tuned in to them.

3. Always keep in mind that what you do for others, you do for Christ. Remember the Scripture that says:

For I was hungry, and you fed me. I was thirsty, and you gave me a drink. I was a stranger, and you invited me into your home.

MATTHEW 25:35

His Princess Love Letter

I believe if your heavenly Father wrote you a personal love letter for today, it would read like this:

Beloved Princess . . .

    If you will refresh others, you will find yourself refreshed. Yes, My beloved, you are called to rescue those who are hurting, but I will go with you and prepare their hearts to receive My love through you. Your heart for the hurting is a reflection of My love for the world. If you look into the eyes of a lost soul, you will see Me. When you feed the hungry, you are feeding Me, your Lord. Remember this, beloved: I did not come for the healthy, I came for the sick and needy. Know this, My Princess, while you are out on the battlefield serving those who cannot serve themselves, I am providing all you need and more!

Love,
  Your King who rescues you

TODAY'S *TREASURE* OF TRUTH

As you are feeding His sheep, He will feed and refresh your soul.

27

OPERATE IN YOUR APPOINTED POSITION TO BE ON CALL

So be on your guard, not asleep like the others. Stay alert and be clearheaded.

1 THESSALONIANS 5:6

One summer evening at our apartment, I went down to our community pool to relax in the Jacuzzi after a long flight home. To my surprise, my relaxation quickly turned into what I call a drunken divine appointment. Two young drunk men and two even drunker young women hopped loudly into my quiet moment. My first thought was to get out and run away to relax somewhere else. However, God captured my heart, and I felt He was asking me to be on call even though I wanted to be on my couch resting. I stayed put and prayed silently, then waited on God to give me my divine assignment.

We started chatting. They began to share all kinds of things with me about their lives, but to be honest I did not tune in to their words because I could hear their hearts cry: "Somebody love me."

Then something happened inside of my exhausted body. My mother's heart gave me the courage and compassion to walk across the hot tub and put my arms around the two girls. I told them how special they were and not to settle for the kind of love that will never last. I looked straight in their eyes and said, "You deserve to be loved."

They said, "Do you think we will ever find someone to really love us?" I asked if I could pray for them. I prayed that God would show them how much He loves them. Then I prayed for their future husbands, and through their drunken tears they hugged me like little girls who needed a spiritual mother.

The boys were watching everything happen, so as I was leaving the hot tub to go home, I looked at them and said, "Be the man you want to be and don't take advantage of girls who are desperate for love." One of the boys said, "You sound like my mother." Then the other boy said, "You sound like my mother too."

Just when I thought my shift to be on call for God was over, the boys began to tell me they were both

Christians who had stopped following Jesus. Both of their moms had been praying for them. It was that moment that tears filled my eyes as I realized I was the answer to a mother's prayers for her son.

I share this story with you to show you that God will call on you if you are willing to be on call.

TODAY'S BIBLE LIFE COACHING

You are called of God every day, and if you're open to answering that call, I would be honored to share some creative ways to hear His voice and allow Him to move through you.

1. Look for those God places in your path who need a little encouragement, or send a quick text or email to a hurting friend. I have even walked by a stranger and just prayed for them without even knowing their need . . . but God heard!
2. Allow God to interrupt your day and embrace those divine interruptions as gifts.

Though I am the least deserving of all God's people, he graciously gave me the privilege of telling the

Gentiles about the endless treasures available to them in Christ.

EPHESIANS 3:8

Women love feeling treasured.

His Princess Love Letter

I believe if your heavenly Father wrote you a personal love letter for today, it would read like this:

Beloved Princess . . .

The time I have given you is of eternal importance. Your life matters, and the most valuable asset you can give to someone or something is time. Remember, My royal one, I want all of your appointments to be in My perfect will. Not all good opportunities are from Me. Keep in mind, My love, that there may be many ways to make more money, but you can never buy back time. So invest your time wisely. Think about what you are doing and how you spend your precious life. Are your days full of the things that matter most to you? Now is the time to take control of your schedule and live a life that matters. If you will sit with Me, I will help you remove the things that are holding you back from doing what's most needed in this season of your life. There is never a wrong time to do the right thing, so come and experience success with divine direction.

Love,
  Your King and eternal Timekeeper

TODAY'S *TREASURE OF TRUTH*

Every day can be an adventure with God if we're not too busy to answer His call.

28

MOVE ON FROM BETRAYAL

As for my companion, he betrayed his friends;
 he broke his promises.
His words are as smooth as butter,
 but in his heart is war.
His words are as soothing as lotion,
 but underneath are daggers!

PSALM 55:20–21

I will never forget sharing tears with women at a retreat where I had been speaking. I had addressed the topic of betrayal during one of my sessions. I saw this woman's pain from across the room. It was as if I knew her story before she shared a word.

Her husband had left her and her four children after fifteen years of marriage. He fell in love with her best friend, so she had been betrayed by the two people she held closest to her heart. I so wanted to find words that could wipe away her pain and give her back her joy. But all I know to do when I can't find a good side to a bad situation is to pray. My prayer came out something like this:

> Dear Jesus,
>
> Please become her best friend and her heavenly husband and the father to her children and the provider of her household. Let her feel Your love with every new day and give her all she needs to feel safe and secure in Your arms, Amen.

To my complete and wonderful surprise, a few months later this woman called me and said that my prayer for her was answered. She began to share that she had experienced God in a way she never would have if she had not lost her husband and best friend to betrayal. She expressed joy as she explained how the hand of God provided for her and her children. She said, "I never really knew how real God was until I walked alone without anyone."

I celebrated with her. Today this woman knows the Lord as her heavenly husband and her healer. Today her faith is in God alone, so it can't be shaken by betrayal.

TODAY'S BIBLE LIFE COACHING

David behaved wisely in all his ways, and the LORD was with him.

1 SAMUEL 18:14 NKJV

I have been working with women for over twenty years, and the chains of pain from betrayal of a loved one or from a fellow Christian are heavy. They seem almost impossible to break. There is a freedom from the heartache of betrayal, but it takes time to heal and wisdom to walk through the recovery process.

David behaved wisely even when Saul betrayed him by turning on him and trying to kill him—the same Saul who once loved David and hosted him in his home.

Joseph shared his dreams with his brothers, but they became jealous and tried to kill his dreams with the weapons of betrayal.

As dreadfully as these two chosen men of God were treated, it was betrayal of man that allowed them to see and experience God in a way they may never have if life had gone differently. The truth is, there is no one we can trust more than God; that said, however, betrayal is still painful.

Betrayal is one of the most painful things to process—that moment when someone you trust with all your heart turns on you or cheats you. How do you recover when a husband walks out on family members? Or someone falsely accuses you of something they did themselves? What about a church friend who breaks your trust and shares your personal struggles with others?

The healing process from betrayal will take some time. But know that just as God was with Joseph in prison and with David in a dark lonely cave, He will be with you. He can and will turn what was intended for evil into good.

The most powerful example of freedom from betrayal is found in the loving, forgiving words of our Lord: When He looked at those who had used and abused Him, then nailed Him to a cross, He said, "Father, forgive them; they know not what they do" (Luke 23:34 KJV).

Your Savior knows your pain. Now let the healing in your heart begin.

His Princess Love Letter

I believe if your heavenly Father wrote you a personal love letter for today, it would read like this:

Beloved Princess . . .

I see you when you are in the garden of grief, My Princess. I hear your cry for help in the dark hours of the night. I Myself cried out in the garden the night I was betrayed. In My suffering I asked My Father for another way—a less painful way. Yet I trusted His will and purpose for My life. I knew the ultimate victory was at the cross. Just as olives must be crushed to make oil, I poured out My life as a love offering for you. Don't ever doubt that I am with you, and that I long to take you to a place of comfort, peace, and victory. Even when you cannot see Me from where you are, I am working on your behalf. Give to Me the crushing weight of your circumstances, and come to Me in prayer. When it is time to leave the garden, I will walk with you across the valley and straight to the cross—where your trials will be transformed into triumph.

Love,

Your Savior and your key to freedom

TODAY'S *T*REASURE OF TRUTH

The best way to protect yourself from allowing betrayal to wipe out your faith is to put your faith only in the One who will never betray you—Jesus.

29

MOVE ON FROM SHAME

Therefore, if anyone is in Christ, he is a new creation;
the old has gone, the new has come!

2 CORINTHIANS 5:17 NIV

Many times we don't feel like a new creation because of hidden shame.

It was twenty-three years ago, and my husband and I were so excited about going to the doctor to confirm that, yes, we were going to have our first baby. There I was, lying on the doctor's table, when he asked me if I wanted to hear my baby's heartbeat. I said, "How is that possible? I'm only six weeks pregnant." I had been told in the past—wrongly!—that babies don't have heartbeats until they are at least twelve weeks in the mother's womb.

The doctor smiled and then placed the stethoscope to my tummy. For the very first time I heard the beat of my son's heart. I began to cry uncontrollably. My husband thought I was crying tears of joy. However, the truth was that I was crying tears of shame and regret.

How could such a miraculous moment bring that reaction? Distant memories flooded my mind. I choked back my tears as I recalled an afternoon twelve years earlier. I was only sixteen at the time, but lying on that doctor's table suddenly made it feel as if it were yesterday. One night when I was desperate for love, I gave up my purity and became pregnant. I was never one to sleep around. It was just once.

Hidden shame many times comes when we least expect it. Often it hits after we've convinced ourselves that one moment of "bad" does not count; after all, we're on track the rest of the time.

Sadly for me, that one moment led me to an abortion doctor who convinced me I was doing the right thing. "It's only been six weeks. It's not a baby," he assured me. "It's a blob. It doesn't even have a heartbeat."

Even though I was not a Christian at the time of my abortion, I was never the same from that moment on. I kept shame hidden inside me after that day.

That shame did not reveal itself in my life in Christ until I was pregnant with my son—and was confronted for the first time with the sad truth about that long-ago decision. I was too ashamed to tell my husband. I even justified that I am a new creation; therefore, that sin must be covered by my Savior without my confession. So I thought.

For several more years I continued to bury that hidden shame, and it turned to intense fear and anxiety that God would take my son in order to punish me. I didn't know how there was any way I could get right with God and be free from something that had happened so long ago.

One Easter weekend in 1999, we went to a Good Friday service at our church. There, displayed in the sanctuary, stood a big wooden cross. As we walked in to worship, each of us was handed a big nail and a small piece of paper. Little did I know that freedom was on its way to my heart that night.

As the pastor told the story of Easter, I embraced it as if I had never heard it before. When he finished, he invited anyone who was holding on to past sin or shame to write it on the paper, walk forward, pick up a hammer, and nail it to the cross.

I sat there paralyzed by my fear of what people would think if I walked forward. After all, I am a woman in leadership, and I thought if I walked forward, it would make God look bad. I struggled with my pride and my deep desire to be free from shame controlling me.

I felt the Spirit of God whisper, *Give Me your past. Give Me your shame.* It took everything in me, but I got up and walked toward the cross. I cried as I picked up that hammer and drove the nail through my confessed sin. I felt the Lord whisper in my spirit, *This is why I had to die for you. So I could take away all your guilt and shame.* At that moment He replaced my past pain with His peace.

I will never be proud of my poor choices. But after that night, I began to understand that confession is more than just something God requires. Confession is a gift from God by which He replaces the strongholds of our past sin and shame with blessings of forgiveness and freedom, healing and hope. Today I am free from the fear of God's punishment, not because of anything I can do in my own power, but because my Lord paid the price for my sin. I am forgiven!

TODAY'S BIBLE LIFE COACHING

Help me abandon my shameful ways;
  for your regulations are good.
I long to obey your commandments!
  Renew my life with your goodness.

PSALM 119:39–40

There is nothing you can do that can keep God from loving or forgiving you.

David loved God with all his heart, but he blew it. He took another man's wife, got her pregnant, then had her husband murdered. He hid behind his sin, thinking it would just go away on its own. But God loved David so much He sent a prophet to confront him so David could be forgiven and freed from shame.

David paid a painful price for what he did when his first son with Bathsheba died. God's grace was with David, however, and the second baby he had with Bathsheba is known today as King Solomon.

Don't wait another day bound up in shame. Whatever makes you ashamed, confess it to your Daddy in heaven and let Him cleanse your soul. Your Father is waiting to free you from shame. He sent His one and only Son to prove His love and to cover our sin, our shame.

We can't make ourselves clean or become a new creation in our own strength. Our loving Father longs to have you confess to Him so He can tenderly cleanse your soul of sin and make you as white as snow.

If you are holding on to something, it's time for you to look at the cross as more than a symbol of your Savior's death. When our Lord died and rose again, He broke forever the power of sin on our lives.

Right now, take a moment to invite the Lord to search your heart for any unresolved sin from your past that continues to torment you. You can experience cleansing and freedom from *this* day forward!

First you start with confession. If confession is something that feels foreign to you, I understand. And I would be honored to lead you in a prayer of confession. Please feel free to make this prayer your very own as you enter God's presence, where chains of shame fall to the ground in His power.

> *Dear God:*
> *I confess _____. I have been hiding*
> *and holding on to this way too long, and I am ready*
> *to be free. I ask Your forgiveness right now, and I*

ask that You help me receive that wonderful gift of
grace You freely give to Your loved ones. I want to
be washed by Your Word and Your Holy Spirit. I
pray this and trust You will complete the process of
my healing and restoration now. Thank You, Lord.
In Jesus' name I pray, Amen.

There is nothing else you need to do right now
except rejoice. Now let faith rule your heart and your
head, and whenever you begin to look back at who
you were or feel shame again, speak out loud, "I am a
new creation." Then continue to ask God to help you
receive all He has for you. You are forgiven whether
you feel like it or not. So embrace it!

His Princess Love Letter

I believe if your heavenly Father wrote you a personal love letter for today, it would read like this:

Beloved Princess . . .

I love it when you come to Me to confess your
sin. I am your safe place and your salvation. There is
nothing you can tell Me that I can't handle hearing.
I already know your every thought and action, so
why waste even a moment trying to hide anything

from Me, My beloved? Let's make it right together. Let Me have the thing that's holding you back from a new and fresh start. Come to Me in truth and be transparent. I'm the Lover of your soul. If you will come to Me and confess, I will gladly wash over your mind, your body, and your spirit to make you clean. You will never need to feel shame again, because I covered you with My life.

Love,
 Your Lord and Savior who died for you

TODAY'S *TREASURE* OF TRUTH

Leave your past where it belongs . . . nailed to the cross!

30

MOVE ONTO
THE BATTLEFIELD

For everything there is a season,
   a time for every activity under heaven.
A time to be born and a time to die.
   A time to plant and a time to harvest. . . .
A time to cry and a time to laugh.
   A time to grieve and a time to dance. . . .
A time to be quiet and a time to speak. . . .
A time for war!

                FROM ECCLESIASTES 3

Have you ever heard the expression "This too shall pass"? My dad used to speak those powerful words, to comfort me when I was walking through a personal battle. Those words still bring me bring me great comfort when life hits hard. King Solomon beautifully reminds us of God's perfect timing in the above Scripture.

Now that I am older, I realize something more—not only that everything will pass, but all I have to hold on to is today. There will never be a season to settle in, and life will always bring unexpected blessings and unexpected battles. So how do we find our way in a world that is so unsettling?

I think one of the hardest things for me is my longing to settle into one season and master the art of living in that season. However, just when my heart seems to settle in, without fail, life brings an unexpected change. Then I find myself feeling frustrated and internally fighting to find a way to embrace a new arena of life. It is not that my life is always hard, but it is always changing, which keeps me in a constant place of surrender to God.

Today I'm learning to embrace every blessing and every battle as they come. Because the truth is, many times in life our circumstances feel like a never-ending battle, and we women grow weary from the fight.

The battlefield is never an easy fight, but the victory is everlasting. Once you have decided to trade your disappointments for His divine appointments, you will begin to see yourself for who you really are—a Princess Warrior and an Ambassador of Hope to the hurting.

It's time to take our blessings and our burdens and use them to become who we want to be: a woman of faith.

The peace, purpose, and passion you are searching for is found on the battlefield. True freedom comes when we surrender our will to God's will and look for ways to further His Kingdom through our imperfect lives. In His power we will not only survive, but we will thrive as His great army.

Let's stop looking for comfort in this life; instead, let's become the comfort this world so desperately needs. Let's take our need to be loved and pour that love into others. Soon the spiritual war will be over, and one day our Lord will wipe away every tear you have cried. He will take you to a place where there is no more pain, no more sickness, no more death. Together we will celebrate your life well-lived, and your faith will never be forgotten!

Until that day, this is your time to turn pain into passion and finish what you were sent here to do. Nothing and no one can cancel out the call of God on your life. He has anointed and appointed you for such a time as this. Your God can use all that you have walked through to prepare you for victory. Don't ever give up your fight, because life is hard. This is your moment to bring a taste of heaven to earth. Don't miss it!

Many times we have to lay down our dreams for divine destiny. Mary could have missed her moment to fight if she had feared what others would think—including her fiancé, Joseph. Mary did not choose to be the birth mother of Jesus. She had to take a step of faith and embrace her calling to receive the blessing of being used to bring heaven to earth.

King David was a mighty warrior of the faith, but his biggest battle was inside himself as he fought to understand why God would choose him. This future king was torn from the many comforts he was accustomed to and forced to hide out in caves to protect his very life. I'm sure David must have wondered, *Is this truly God's will for my life?*

King David did not ask God to become a leader of the faith, but David did say yes to the call to fight to further God's Kingdom. It took sixteen years of "spiritual boot camp," personal battles, and great sacrifices to prepare David to lead God's people.

David did not allow the battles to make him bitter; instead he transferred his painful preparation time into prayers and cried out to God in writing. Today those pain-filled prayers found in the book of Psalms show us how to find God in our own personal battles. His calling was not easy, but his life was full of adventure and his faith still lives on in our hearts today.

TODAY'S BIBLE LIFE COACHING

I know it is hard to see yourself as a David or a Mary, but they are really no different from you and me. They were imperfect people who stepped out and trusted God by surrendering their will to God's will for their lives. They lost much, but they gained a legacy of faith. They fought to walk the narrow road, trusting their God to guide them all the way home to heaven.

Don't miss out on the amazing adventure awaiting you. Get up and get on the battlefield where your legacy of faith is waiting for you. As you step forward and find the courage you need, I want you to think on this Scripture:

For the LORD your God is going with you! He will fight for you against your enemies, and he will give you victory!

DEUTERONOMY 20:4

Now I leave you with this final love letter. I believe it will help you remember your Father is fighting on your behalf. You can confidently place your hand in His and dance on any battlefield He places you on in this life!

His Princess Love Letter

I believe if your heavenly Father wrote you a personal love letter for today, it would read like this:

Beloved Princess . . .

I have created a time for every season of life. My timing is perfect for every plan I have. Right now, My beloved, it is a time for you to get dressed for spiritual battle, because you are more than a princess—you are "My Princess Warrior." I am going with you onto the battlefield, and in those times you feel as if there is no fight left inside of you, My Spirit will rise up inside your soul. My strength will become your strength. My mighty armor will guard your heart from the fiery arrows of the enemy. In the power of My Holy Spirit, you will find the passion and power to step out in faith and face any spiritual giant that comes against you.

Your battles won for My Kingdom will become a blessing to all generations!

Love,
 Your King who fights for you

TODAY'S *TREASURE* OF TRUTH

It is in the heat of a battle we have the chance to show a "real faith" that can't be seen through the eyes of man but through the faith of His people.

A FINAL WORD
FROM SHERI ROSE . . .

As we close our thirty days together, I pray that you have found your desire to dance in freedom. I pray from this day forward you find joy in knowing you are the Lord's. I pray you embrace every new trial as a test of your faith and a way to show the world your faith.

If I never meet you here on earth, I so look forward to celebrating your life lived for Him when we reach heaven.

SHERI ROSE

Sheri Rose Shepherd is the bestselling author of *His Princess, His Princess Bride, Fit for My King*, and several other books. She is a popular speaker and Bible teacher, and her teaching was the number one show of the year on *Focus on the Family*. Her life story about overcoming her struggles with weight problems, dyslexia, and depression has been featured on the *Billy Graham Primetime Television Special*.

Join Best-selling Author & Speaker

Sheri Rose Shepherd

for Online Mentoring,
Video Teaching and more at

BibleLifeCoaching.com

Bring your friends! Each Week You Will Find...

- *All New and Fresh Online Video*
- *Amazing Worship Songs from Top Artists*
- *Bible-Life Coaching & Application*
- *Treasures of Truth*
- *Personal Prayers for you*
- *A message board for comments & discussion*

 @BibleCoaching

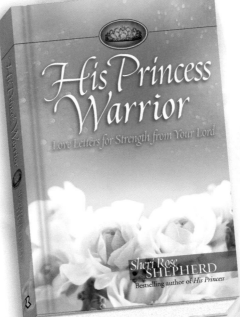

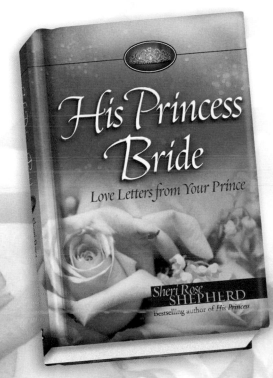

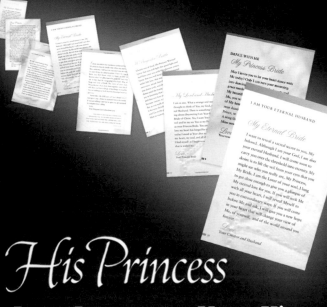

His Princess

Love Letters from Your King

E-mailed to You Each Weekday!

visit HisPrincess.com
or connect with Sheri Rose Shepherd on Facebook